Real Love Stories Never Have Endings

After Death Communication and Other Messages from Beyond

Beatrice D. Marx

Beatrice Marx

Copyright © 2014 Beatrice Marx
All rights reserved.

ISBN: ISBN-13: 978-0615980850

ISBN-10: 0615980856

Real Love Stories Never Have Endings

This book is dedicated to all those who wish they could still be with their departed loved ones, so that they rejoice and know that their loved ones are still around.

Beatrice Marx

Contents

PREFACE	7
PART I – After Death Communication	13
CHAPTER 1 – When It All Began	15
CHAPTER 2 – I See Ghosts	23
CHAPTER 3 – And I Hear Them Too	29
CHAPTER 4 – My Dad	37
CHAPTER 5 – My Mom	47
CHAPTER 6 – The Love of My Life	65
CHAPTER 7 – The Power of Dreams	73
CHAPTER 8 – Messages from the Other Side	79
CHAPTER 9 – The Angel of Love	85
CHAPTER 10 – The Power of Love	89
CHAPTER 11 – The Purpose of Communication	95
PART II – Ethereal Messages for the Good of the Universe	
CHAPTER 12 – Visions and Previsions	107
CHAPTER 13 – Planetary Healer	113
CHAPTER 14 – Heal the Water	123

CHAPTER 15 – We Are All Divine	129
CHAPTER 16 – Scientific Vindication	139
CHAPTER 17 – The Fifth World	143
EPILOGUE	153
NOTES	155
ABOUT THE AUTHOR	157

Preface

A few months ago, my uncle passed away. He was the last link with my mother and with the past generation that leaves room for the next. He lived in Normandy, where I was born and grew up, and where all my ancestors lived, as far back as we can go in archival times, to the 16th century. The day of his funeral, I was paddling my kayak on one of the many lakes of Seattle, enjoying the peace and the beauty of the early morning, when the water is smooth and wildlife timidly shows up, making sure that no humans have invaded their territory.

I wanted to be with him in thought since the distance did not allow me to attend in person. It was a special moment, enjoying the serenity of the moment and wishing him farewell on his journey back home where I knew he would be greeted by many friends and family members.

Suddenly, a song overwhelmed me and before I knew it, I was singing it out loud, breaking the silence of that peaceful early morning. It was a song I used to sing on Sundays at the Protestant church of my home town, which my uncle attended, and where he was being honored one last time by those who loved him. The following day, I called my sister to ask for news and about the service, and I asked her if they had sung during the ceremony that special song I had been drawn to sing; she confirmed that indeed they did. I knew that my uncle had received my wishes of love and farewell when he sent this song my way.

People who pass away do not leave us. They remain among us forever and can, and do, communicate with us.

When I relayed this story to his son, he asked me when "it" all started, "it" being my communication with the world on the other side. I remember well when it started. And since that day, it has only increased in power, clarity and frequency. We are not alone; we are never left alone; those who have left us go on loving us beyond the frontier of the visible world.

This book is dedicated to all those who wish they could still be with their departed loved ones, so that they rejoice and know that their loved ones are still around.

Many events have occurred since the first day it began, when I was just a little girl. Since then, I have had a lot of communication with loved ones, and even a few physical encounters with unknown ghosts. Over the years, I have felt emotions ranging from surprise, fear, disbelief, thankfulness, openness, addiction, greed for more, love, understanding, respect, acceptance, impatience for meeting with them again, sorrow, joy, and comfort. When I go back and look at all these messages and communications, I feel that their comforting presence has always been here, and will always be, and it is great to know that. They are not gone, they are just on a journey in higher, invisible spheres, and sometimes, they do stop by to say hi.

I started researching these phenomena in 1998 after my mom passed away. Soon after her death, amazing communication occurred that could not be left unexplored. I began to read every book I could find on the topic, I researched similar events in history, I browsed blogs on line that recounted of similar events, and I met with people who seemed to already be connected with the world I was eager to discover.

I wanted to open my mind and understand. I wanted to discover the unknown. The more I learned, the more there was to learn. One story led to another. I was amazed and fascinated. I discovered that similar experiences occurred as far back as antiquity and before, and that history had both accepted and condemned such connections. And today, a revival is underway, which I believe can be explained by a new consciousness and the reopening of our third eye and of the connection paths between our world and the other side. Forty years ago, talking about spirits and messages with the invisible world was considered taboo or crazy and even more so in France where I come from; then, several years ago, I felt it appeared fine to talk about it; I was no longer considered a lunatic or a witch.

So, little by little, everything made sense, until I reached a point of complete awareness of our common thread, a spiritual connection that is infinite between this world and the other side. This thread extends from before we come on earth as an embodied spirit and continues after we depart, when we leave our envelope and go back to the spirit world. No beginning, no end, infinite connection. And it is all about love. Not only love as we usually know it, but an unconditional, pure love for all living beings on earth, including trees, streams, fish, birds, our entire environment and those who inhabit it, and spirits, entities from the other side, angels, souls of our loved ones who went back home, the whole Universe to which we all belong.

And when I reached the point of awareness of being one with the Universe, I started receiving more messages directly related to the earth and its great need for help, a plea for salvation. And I learned that we can indeed save the earth and help it by sending her vibrations of love like the ones we receive from our loved ones from the other side. We need to honor and love the earth as we honor and cherish our loved ones; through this radiation of love around us, we can help the earth go through this traumatic transition it is now going through, after all the abuse it has been suffering from humans. Because what comes through these messages is nothing else but Divine Love, ready for us to share.

Since 1998 when I started researching the subject, I have noticed that communication has become more frequent not only for me, but for many people. I think indeed that communication is not reserved to only a few, but it is open to all who are ready and willing to open their minds and receive these messages of love, without any preconceived ideas or doubts about their reality.

Nothing is forced upon us, but whenever a soul is open to this divine love, it is one more soul working toward the good of our universe. I have been blessed to be a receiver and a conveyor of messages from the other side and I know that it is all for global wellbeing, our healing as embodied souls, and the healing of the earth. My research confirmed that indeed all the communications I have received over the years are part of a great scheme toward the new paradigm, a world of love and common work toward harmony and peace.

Real Love Stories Never Have Endings

Beatrice Marx

Real Love Stories Never Have Endings

PART ONE

AFTER DEATH COMMUNICATION

Beatrice Marx

1

When It All Began

It all started when I was eleven years old. I was living with my parents in the family house that my paternal grand-father had built in the early 1900's. It was a large two-story house built in stones and bricks, with a garden where my grand-father grew apples and made cider. They had ten children but three passed away as toddlers during the big flu epidemic of 1918. Three girls and four boys remained; one was mentally disabled. My father was the youngest. My grand-father passed away when I was three and my grand-mother lived in the house with her disabled son until she passed away in 1969.

When my grand-mother passed away, my disabled uncle lost the support he required; he could not live on his own. So, the six brothers and sisters met and discussed the situation. None of them wanted to take their brother to live with them. It was indeed a huge responsibility and commitment to care for a disabled adult man. He was like a child, nice, smiling, quiet, very respectful and obedient, but did not know the reality of life. He required supervision and direction constantly, in addition to food, shelter and love. The solution the family came to was to put him in a long term facility for disabled people and sell the family house. At that time we were living in Tours, in the Loire Valley. My dad worked in a furniture store and my mother in an office. My parents liked it there; they had friends and enjoyed spending time in the countryside with them. They were loving parents.

Life for them was about having good times, having fun and enjoying life. Some of their friends had a farm and a vineyard that yielded an excellent white wine of Touraine. While they were enjoying the fruits of the vines, I enjoyed the bucolic life of the countryside. I fed the pigs with the farmer, ran in the fields in the summer, fished in the pond, and played with the kids from the neighboring farm.

However, when my paternal grand-mother passed away and the dilemma of "what to do with my uncle" occurred, it did not take long for my parents to make their decision. They had more heart than money. My mother was heartbroken to imagine that he would be put in an "inhumane" environment –as she would say- where he would surely die of sadness. She knew how my grand-mother felt about what would happen to my uncle after she passed away and there was no way she would dishonor her mother in law's last wish. She did not hesitate and told my father that they should move in the family house in Le Havre and take care of my uncle. I was only eleven at that time but I remember conversations and what she later told me about how important it was for my grand-mother to know that her son would be well taken care of. Thus, we left our apartment in Tours and moved in the family home in Le Havre in the summer of 1969.

The house was still like my grand-father had built it, with no modern amenities. It was a two-story house with a basement accessible by stairs dug in the ground. It was cold and dark and was used as a storage room by my grand-mother before refrigerators existed. I was fascinated by it. The rough walls were cold and slimy and I was careful to stay away from them. My dad told me that as a kid, he spent some time there when punished by his mom.

My grand-mother "was not all sweet" as my mom used to tell me. But to her defense, life was tough with seven kids to raise and feed. There was no bathroom and no toilet, and an old coal stove was used to heat the house as well as cook the meals. My dad used to tell us and show us how my grand-father would take a hot coal directly from the stove to light his cigarette, telling us how his fingertips were covered with calluses from working hard at the foundry. As for toilets, we still had to go outside in the garden and use the wooden toilet bowl in a small shack that my dad would empty in the yard every few months. Our flowers grew well in the garden!

My older sister shared a room with my older brother, probably because they were closer in age. My bedroom was a former closet that my dad had converted into a room for me. It had a tall window that overlooked the garden. Both ends of my bed touched the walls of my room and dad set up a foldable table on the side wall so that I could do my homework sitting on the bed. He also put some golden metallic shelves above my bed and I also had a small bedside table where I put my record player. I was really excited and proud of having my own room. Though it was very small, it was my own private place; it was my secret garden. I put all of my books and trinkets on the shelves, including a broken alarm clock that belonged to my maternal grandmother. It was a pale green alarm clock, the kind that you could hear ticking so loudly that it could wake up an army. She would never go anywhere without it and she always told me that the day she passed away, I could have it. When she died in 1968, my mother gave it to me. Unfortunately it broke not long after I got it, but I decided to keep it and put it on my shelf anyway.

I began a habit of saying good night to my grand-mother every evening while looking at the clock and talking to her in my head. Then one evening, while I was talking to her as I did so often, her alarm clock rang, loudly and bright. It was my first encounter with telepathic thoughts from the other side. I was puzzled. I could not believe my ears. I was also very happy but it was difficult for me to understand how it could have happened. I remember that I took the alarm clock in my hands, turned it around, put it by my ear to see if it was ticking, tried rewinding it, excited at the idea that it would work again, but nothing happened. The mechanism was still stuck and the alarm clock was still broken. I suddenly realized that my grand-mother had received my message and was responding to it. It was exhilarating. It was my first communication with the other side.

While this event was first hand communication, I also had the opportunity, during the same period of time, to hear a story that triggered even more curiosity.

I was a girl scout at that time. We used to spend some week-ends in the countryside, hiking in the country roads of Normandy and sleeping in hay barns. We used to talk a lot in the evening and we enjoyed this time of sharing stories. One evening, one of my leaders told us the story of her grand-mother who had passed away and who would regularly walk by the window of their kitchen. They could also hear her in the attic moving pans and making noise. It was fascinating. Ghost stories that really existed! I remember thinking that since these incidents involved loving family members, such ghosts could not be scary or mean. I could imagine the scene of her grand-mother walking by the kitchen window during dinner while all her family was sitting at the table. Her grand-mother probably missed the family times she used to share and cooking for all. From that day forward, I wished it would happen to me and that someday I could see ghosts.

While my girl scout's leader's stories were exciting and positive, my mother told me we should not explore the other side. She told me with wide open eyes and a respectful stare that black magic existed, that it could be dangerous and that we should stay away from it. She would tell me of a very old friend of her mom named Melanie who she suspected did black magic. She explained that once, when she went to clean Melanie's apartment, she found a tray with candles and other objects that looked like they were used for rituals hidden behind a dresser.

I remember going to visit this woman a few times. She was a small, frail, very old woman with long curly hair. She was almost completely blind and the veins of her skin showed through her translucent skin. I was very intimidated by her looks and her voice and the stories that my mother told me about her, so when visiting her, I always held my mother's hand and looked at the dresser and around the small apartment, looking for some magic, for the tray and candles that my mom had told me about. I would have never touched anything in her apartment, maybe for fear of receiving a bad spell. However she liked me and always took my hand in hers. I remember the touch of her hands on mine and the sound of her tiny, crystalline voice. I was fascinated by the idea that she could contact the other side.

My mother's warnings about the dark side of black magic created in me a feeling of respect and caution; however, I still wanted to know more about the other side and this huge, mysterious and forbidden world. I did not know anything about the life of this old woman who probably had loved many people. Maybe she was merely communicating with her departed loved ones and trying to restore the thread of love with those who were gone, or maybe she was simply doing black magic.

In the late 1960s, the concept of communicating with dead people had a scary and negative connotation; it was something done by witches and warlocks. So, between my leader's story and Melanie, I had two representations of the other side. On one hand was the direct communication with loved ones, through totally unexplainable events such as making a broken clock work, or a dead person appear as if alive, and on the other hand, the unknown world of black magic with spells and a potential danger of unknown nature, which I imagined from the forbidden world hidden behind Melanie's dresser. Both seemed magic to me and inspired great curiosity in the mind of the little girl I was.

Many more events followed. And except for a few instances of very unexpected, unnerving encounters, none involved bad spirits or witchcraft, only spirits of loving people who had passed away, mostly family.

As I explained earlier, my parents had made the decision to come and live in the family house in order to take care of my disabled uncle when my paternal grand-mother passed away. The house was still as my grand-father had built it; there were no new amenities, and the wallpaper seemed to date from the beginning of the century. I liked that house; it felt home. Then, one morning, several months after we had moved in, my mother told us that in the middle of the night, she woke up and saw my grand-mother standing on her side of the bed. She was looking at her and then simply disappeared. It happened two or three times in all. I believe my grand-mother wanted to acknowledge my mother for taking care of my uncle.

As a little girl, it started to become part of reality. I did not question it. It was now an evident fact that people who passed away did not go away. I did not question it. It was actually quite awesome to realize that loved ones were not completely gone, that they still remained among us, but in different ways. My personal experience later confirmed that they do remain around, always ready to show up whenever we feel down or need comfort. In the years that followed, all communication with loved ones and even with unknown spirits and beings of light, occurred when I had sent an invitation, many times subconsciously, for communication, or better said, for love, comfort, or just a simple request for a hi! from the other side.

My family house was certainly haunted by my grand-parents. In addition to the episodes when my grand-mother appeared to my mom, several unusual events occurred in my bedroom. They all happened at night and after a while I did not try to find an explanation for them. I knew it was part of the unexplainable magic of the world from the other side.

Several nights I was awaken by my turntable playing music. At the time we did not have electronics or CD players. I had an old record player that you had to manually trigger to make work. And it happened on its own, playing a record that I had left on the turntable the day before. That was puzzling indeed, but I never felt endangered or scared. I just wished that someday I could see these ghosts that were playing around in my bedroom. By then, I knew that both my grand-mothers had showed up to express their love and confirm that they were around, which was really comforting.

2

I See Ghosts

In 1974, I went to London for several months as an au-pair, as it was quite common at that time for young Europeans who wanted to learn English. I came back to France at the end of spring and went to Southern France to work in the corn fields with a friend I met in England. We had a great time and got along well.

After working for a month in the field, we decided to go to Spain hitchhiking. We had an amazing time, two young girls on a road trip to wherever the wind would take us in Spain. Franco was still the head of the country and it was risky for two girls to go there. However we did it, probably because we did not know of the dangers of that time.

One day, as we were heading out of Madrid, our thumbs up and smiles on our faces, a huge truck stopped and a handsome young Spanish man with curly black hair who reminded me of Julio Iglesias, whom I loved!, asked us where we were going. We told him that we were on our way to Barcelona and he offered us a ride. Since I spoke Spanish, it helped a lot and we immediately got along well. He told us that he owned his truck and had a few days ahead of him before his next shipment, and he offered to show us around. What was supposed to be a one day ride became several days of pure bliss. We had a delightful time; sun, sea, laughs, conversations, sightseeing.

Not long after we had met, we got attracted to each other and a summer love story started, a fling where you hold hands and kiss, talk a lot, laugh, and giggle. It was so enjoyable! Once in Tarragona he had to go his way and we had to go ours, but we kept in touch. One year later, I decided to go to Barcelona to study Spanish. Once I was settled in town, I contacted Manolo and he came to visit me as soon as he could.

We soon became lovers and we very much enjoyed the company of each other. Since he was from Madrid, I would see him from time to time when his work would take him to the coast. In the winter of that year, he told me that he had a load to drive to Holland and he asked me if I would want to go with him and stop on the way to see my parents in Le Havre. I was thrilled. So we left Barcelona in his big truck and went on the road.

It was a long way to Holland and we stopped a few times on the way. His truck had a cabin to sleep in, so while he was driving and the evening was getting long, I would sometimes go in the back and rest. One evening, as he wanted to cover some miles and it was already dark and late, I went in the cabin behind him and fell asleep. The curtains were half open and my head was on the side of the driver, so I could see from where I was the right side of the road passing by rather than the lights of the cars from the other side.

At some point, Manolo stopped the truck in a rest area for coffee. The silence and lack of motion of the vehicle soon woke me up and I opened my eyes. On each side of me three people were staring down at me. They did not do anything other than look at me. I remember, one of these people was a young woman in her thirties with short dark hair. I did not feel threatened, just surprised. I could see between two of them the dark night outside of the cabin and it was obvious that they were lost. They looked stuck, not knowing what they were doing, wondering what I was doing there, maybe thinking that I was now part of their world, since in our sleep is when we are the closest to the energy field of spirits. They did not move; they just looked at me, all six pairs of eyes on me, and then they left as they had come.

Subsequent research confirmed indeed instances in which spirits of people who die in dramatic and sudden circumstances stay around the location of their death because they are not aware they are dead, which could explain ghost stories, and definitely the visit I had that night.

A few years ago, I had the opportunity to have a vision of a ghost again, but this time, it had the appearance of a human being. Instead of a floating shape, it was like watching a third dimensional scene not visible to the common eye, yet real in a different dimension. Just imagine putting on glasses that would enable you to see elements that you could not see with the naked eye, yet that still existed. It is what happened on the very sad day of my best friend's son funeral.

My best friend's son was killed in action in Afghanistan in 2008. It was devastating. The day of the funeral, Seattle's cathedral was crowded, representatives of the army were numerous, and a lot of intense emotion filled the cathedral. I was so sad for my friend. When all had entered the cathedral and the ceremony began, the bearer came in. I expected to see six men in uniform formally bearing a long casket covered with the American flag, but instead, one man came in, holding in his hand a small wooden box that contained the ashes of my friend's son. In France where I am from, bodies are cremated *after* the ceremony, thus I was rather shocked to see this small wooden box for such a dramatic event. It seemed surreal. The music was playing, friends, family and brothers in combat were all gathered for him, but he was not there. The emotion was so intense that I could not feel anything other than pain, the pain and sorrow of my friend who looked like a lost, little bird, so frail, so fragile. She was not there either. She was with her son, in thoughts and almost in body.

The burial ceremony followed. A hole had been dug, a small table set up, the family was standing in line, ready to receive the American flag from the hands of army officials. The emotion was dissipated in the fresh air. But my friend was still looking as if she were living an out-of-body experience. Her eyes were fixated on the small table and the small box that contained her son's ashes. Her facial expression was surreal. Her eyes were disconnected from reality. I felt her pain and deep sorrow. I wanted to comfort her but I could not. This moment was hers to live in intense, unspeakable sorrow and pain.

I followed the direction of her eyes toward the small table, and there he was. Sitting on the table, his legs crossed and swinging back and forth, with a relaxed and laid back look of peace on his face, he was watching his own burial. I had met him only once so I did not know him other than from what my friend told me, mostly about the fact that he was a free spirit who enjoyed his encounters with the Afghan people, which he documented with amazing photos of a very strong human dimension. I did not know his personality. But there he was. Was he trying to convey supportive feelings to his mom? Or enjoying the gathering of all his friends and family? I don't know but there he was.

The little wooden box did not have much importance in this whole picture. He was there, fully present. I wanted to tell my friend "Look! He is here! He is ok! He doesn't want you to be sad", but I could not, since the ceremony was still on. But it was so intense. And the feelings that were emanating from each of them were the total opposite. He was so laid back, swinging his legs back and forth, with a peaceful face, and his mom was lost, distraught, her eyes lost in the beyond, in another space.

Several weeks later, when I saw my friend, I told her about what happened that day and I described to her the scene, her son's behavior and the feelings that were emanating from him that day. She was really happy and told me that she recognized her son's behavior in my description. It would have been just the way he would have viewed his own funeral.

Beatrice Marx

3

And I Hear Them Too

One of my passions is running rivers with my inflatable kayak for several days at a time. I pack food, water, shelter, and ride the rivers, away from civilization, paddling smoothly and enjoying every moment; the tortoise gliding back into the water, the deer drinking at the edge of the river in the early morning, the bees that stop by, curious to see what is out there in the middle of the river, and the birds that sometimes accompany me for a few hundred yards before flying away.

Late August of 2011, I decided to explore a section of the Upper Missouri River, between Coal Banks Landing and Kipp Recreation Area, which covers 107 miles of gorgeous scenery. In addition to being a beautiful section of the Missouri river, with the White Cliffs and its canyon, which Meriwether Lewis described as "scenes of visionary enchantment," this section of the river has a historical component that adds even more interest to the trip. Markers along the river show where Lewis and Clark stopped and camped on their expedition, with some quotes from their journal. I had stopped in Great Falls on my way to the put in to visit the Lewis and Clark Interpretive Center where they narrate the expedition and show a replica of their huge, heavy, dugout canoe, so, while paddling, I thought about these men and how easy I had it, compared to them, with my inflatable kayak, dry bags, bug repellent, and food from the store.

Yet, while Lewis and Clark's expedition is fascinating, another episode of history also took place on this river, which was even more special to me, not only because I have a very strong interest in the history of American Indians, but also because it involved injustice and violence, which are against my core, intrinsic values, and I feel deep compassion for these people who suffered so much when the whites came and took over their land.

On September 23, 1877, Chief Joseph and his people crossed the river at Cow Island at river mile 127 and camped up the creek for two days. Their march was following negotiations about having to give up their territory of the Wallowa Valley to the whites and go and live on a small reservation in Idaho. Several events led to battles, gunfire, wounded and dead soldiers, civilians, and Indians, and they were now fleeing the army and going toward Canada, in the hope of meeting their friend Sitting Bull and living peacefully with the Sioux. At the same time, soldiers were stationed in Cow Island, guarding food supplies that had been unloaded off steamboats, and the Nez Perce, who were exhausted from their journey fleeing the army and starving, asked the soldiers for some food. While they did get some, it was not enough; further exchanges did not go very well; gunfire occurred, and civilians and Indians were wounded.

Chief Joseph[1] and about four hundred men, women, and children, hungry, cold, and exhausted from a seventeen hundred mile marching over a period of three months, and enduring several battles with the army, surrendered twelve days later. As I had studied their story while at the University, I was particularly interested in this episode of history and thought a lot about their suffering, and all these women and children dying from cold and exhaustion.

It was about three in the afternoon while I was paddling and thinking about this part of history. The sky ahead of me was nice and clear, but as the ranger had warned me before I had left on my trip, clouds and thunder on this river always come from behind. So, while paddling, I always had to look behind my shoulder to make sure all was well.

While turning around to see the sky, I saw a dark black wall in the background. Sure enough a storm was approaching. A few minutes later I started hearing the thunder rumbling. I knew I did not have much time to get out of the water before it would hit. I had to paddle fast before reaching the next sand and gravel bar. A few minutes later, I landed, pulled my boat out of the water on higher grounds, unloaded as fast as I could, set up my tent in a record time, jumped inside, zipped up the zipper, and heard the first two drops of rain on my tent.

I felt relieved to be dry and all my gear secured. Storms on the Upper Missouri River are like I have never seen in my life. They are violent, the rain hits hard and heavy, the sky is black, and the thunder loud. It lasted for about half an hour, until the sky finally cleared up, leaving an amazing colorful and magical scene, with hues in the blues, pinks, and oranges. It was gorgeous. I emerged out of my tent and looked at the peaceful scene, after having witnessed one of the most violent storms I had ever experienced. An eagle flew in front of me above the water, and the smell of the wet grass was emanating from the ground. It was extremely peaceful and blissful to be there; unique and memorable moments that make such trips priceless.

Then, all of a sudden, I heard people singing. In the middle of the silence of this area where no road access to the river exists, I could hear people sing. I walked along the small stretch where I had set up my tent, trying to see where these voices were coming from, thinking that maybe on the other side there were people in canoes, which was quite unlikely since I had only seen three canoes since I had left Coal Bank Landings four days before. I went in the direction of the sounds and I realized that these were Indian songs; while no one was to be seen, songs were sung; songs with a strong, deep voice, and intonations unique to Indians. I was mesmerized. I looked at the guidebook[2] and the boater's guide from the Bureau of Land Management that I used along my trip and I realized that the spot where I had landed in emergency was close to mile 127, a few hundred yards from Cow Creek, where Chief Joseph had camped for three days after their extenuating march, starving and cold, just a few days before they had to sadly surrender.

I had goose bumps all over my body and tears in my eyes. Could these songs be from those men who had lost their battle for freedom 134 years ago? I sent them my love and honored them for their courage. In spirit they were still mourning, or maybe still fighting, or hoping for freedom and peace. These songs were very powerful. I stood there, listening to them, taken over by the strength of the emotion that emanated from it. I was in contemplation, sharing the moment with them in thought. It lasted just a few minutes and then it was gone.

Silence was back on the river. I had tears in my eyes. I had just been a part of history, feeling the human trauma of a people. Past and present occurring at the same time through an everlasting connecting thread; their energy was still around. While their bodies were long gone, they were still there in spirit. I had heard of instances where ghosts said a few words, but that experience was overwhelming in beauty and realization that linear time was not applying to such experiences. Past and present were happening at the same time.

When someone from the past acts in the present, I wonder, are these people in a parallel world living their own reality in their present time? Or coming back? Or did they ever leave?

I had another opportunity to wonder the same question a few months later.

In the little town of Edmonds, close to where I live in the State of Washington, is a historical museum. The town of Edmonds was created in 1884 by George Brackett, a logger in search of timber. It is situated on the beautiful shores of the Puget Sound, and since 1884, the city has been expanding on its hills, while still keeping its atmosphere of a small town where it feels good hanging out, exploring its art galleries, having coffee in local coffee shops and enjoying the summer market on Saturdays.

As I was walking by the museum on a spring day, I decided to go and visit it. I climbed the few stairs to the entrance and opened the door. A young woman was standing there and no other visitors were to be seen. I paid the entrance fee and started looking at the exhibits. I soon arrived in front of a room that looked like a Victorian parlor, set up with original furnishings, framed pictures, lamps, a rocking chair and a small table next to it.

I immediately felt the presence of someone. It was as if the person had just left the chair to get a cup of tea and was going to be back soon. I asked the receptionist who the furniture belonged to and she told me that they had been donated by Zenna E. Cook, the daughter of Mayor William H. Cook, the first mayor of the town. I stayed for a few minutes, looking at every item. A very nice and warm atmosphere emanated from this room. A thick, red velvet cord was hanging from one side of the door to the other one and a pulpit was standing in front of the room to prevent people from entering it and disturbing the peace of a moment frozen in time. I really felt that the lady to whom this furniture belonged was there. I did not move or make any noise as I wanted to soak in this peaceful atmosphere. I stood there, looking at the rocking chair where I could really feel a presence. I thanked in thoughts the lady for sharing her beautiful belongings. To my surprise, the wooden pulpit in front of me moved down and up, and the lights in the room went off. After a few seconds of surprise, I realized that she was there, as I had felt it. I responded that I was happy that she acknowledged my thanks and I wished her well. It was a very nice and peaceful moment of connection.

I turned around and went to see the lady at the reception desk. I told her: "you know that you are not alone, right?" and I told her about what had just happened. And she responded: "yes, I know!" and she turned the lights back on.

Beatrice Marx

4

My Dad

My dad was born in 1930 in a French middle class family. He was the youngest of seven siblings and was raised in the two-story family home that my grand-father had built in one of the uptown neighborhoods of Le Havre in Normandy until he married my mother at the age of twenty. He was a wonderful man, very resourceful and courageous. He worked hard for his family and was a grounded, strong willed man. He was a role model to me. He did not talk much which made conversations with him even more precious.

I loved it when he told us stories about his youth. He told us about his mother and how she handled the household, how discipline was part of their life, and how important family values were. With seven siblings and one salary that my grand-father brought back home, it was hard to feed the whole family but she made it work. He also told us about World War II. At that time he was a young boy and like most people he was hungry "because the Germans took everything" as he told us, so one evening, he went with a friend of his and sneaked in a German camp to steal food and chocolate. He described how they could hear and see the Germans, how they were hiding in the night and felt so happy when they managed to get some food and a piece of chocolate from them. It sounded like a teenage adventure, but it was a dangerous one and it could have cost them their lives. They were aware of it but they had a hard time dealing with the occupation of their home land and the hunger in their stomachs, and this daring action was his way of dealing with it.

It was fascinating to imagine him sneaking into this camp, fearless and brave, as young people can be. This German camp was located in a small pedestrian street linking uptown to downtown that I took every day to go to school, and every day, I tried to imagine the scene of the Germans talking loud, smoking, and laughing, and my father and his friend surreptitiously sneaking in behind the bushes and taking food from them. It always brought a smile to my face, and made me proud to be his daughter.

He was also so proud telling us how he built his first bicycle from parts that he gathered one by one and paid for by selling ice cream. He found some canvas and sewed satchels for it. He always loved riding his bicycle and he even won cycling races. He told us how he knew Jacques Anquetil, a famous French cyclist who won numerous Tour de France events, and how they used to bike together when he was young.

He knew the value of hard work, the value of having food on your plate and a roof above your head, and he worked hard all his life to provide for our family. He was a jack of all trades, able to make anything with whatever he found. A broken piece of furniture would become new again under his agile hands; he built a doll house for my sister and even sewed a leather coat for her Barbie doll.

His craftsmanship equaled his life skills. There was nothing he could not solve, not a tricky situation he could not find a positive way out. While he did not go farther than elementary school as it was quite common in post-war Europe where only the oldest son of a family was sent to college, he was a self-taught man. What he knew, he shared with us; as an adult, I was lucky to live next to my parents and I got to spend time with them quite often. My dad was proud of his family. He had a picture of me in his wallet taken when I was nineteen and he always showed it to new acquaintances and people at work. I silently worshiped him as my hero, the man who could do it all, the man who had a solution to any problem or question. The man who was always there for me whenever I felt down. He was a loving father.

Then, during family meals in the mid-1990s, my dad started mentioning that he would never see the year 2000. He was born in 1930 and it sounded bizarre to say such a thing since he was in good health and would only be seventy in the year 2000, yet he was convinced that he would be dead by then. He would joke and say: "By the year 2000, I will have started eating dandelions by the root!"

I was always sad when he would say that because I loved him so much, and I did not want to even think about the day he would leave us. I remember at that time I had remarried and I lived happily in a nice little house in Southern France. My third daughter was still an infant and we enjoyed Sunday lunches together gathered around the family table. We laughed a lot and spent hours around the table eating, chatting, laughing, drinking refreshing rosé wine from the local wineries. It was a very nice time in my life.

In the summer of 1996, my dad came to see me at home and told me that he was not feeling well. He did not want to worry my mother but it seemed that he was forgetting things; he knew that there was something wrong. He told me that it was probably the age and that we should not worry too much. However, since my dad was not the kind to elaborate on his health, it was concerning to me that he would share this with me. It was the first time that he actually did.

A few weeks later, in September of 1996, my parents went to Spain on vacation for a week. They were driving to the Costa Brava, not far from the French/Spanish border where they had booked an all-inclusive week in a hotel by the beach. The day after their arrival there, I received a phone call from my mother. She told me that there was something wrong with my father, he showed some strange physical reactions and could neither drive nor walk straight. She was so concerned that she called the family doctor and they had to be repatriated from Spain.

In the days that followed, my dad underwent several tests at the local hospital. From a blood test to a scan, within a few days the doctors found what was wrong. My brother called me at home one late afternoon and told me that they had the results of the tests. Dad had a brain tumor the size of a grapefruit and they gave him six months to live. It was the most devastating news in my whole life. I was in shock and not able to quite assimilate what I was hearing. It could not be.

My dad, my hero, the man who was able to solve anything, to get out of any situation, my dad who was so healthy, riding his bicycle every weekend, who was always bragging about the fact that he had the heart of a twenty year old man, as his doctor would tell him each year before he would give him his agreement to participate in bicycle races, my dad was facing something that he could not solve. He was going to die. It was not acceptable. At that time I was training for a new job and scheduled to go to Paris for several weeks but I canceled my trip to stay next to my parents. I went to see my father every day in the hospital and day by day, I saw him lose his physical and mental abilities. Less than two months after he was diagnosed, he passed away. I was so angry with God, I did not want to hear about him any longer. He had taken my dad away. It was the most unbearable event in my life.

My dad had always told me that there was a solution to any problem. He was resourceful, courageous, strong, healthy, and here we were, in the hospital room, a few weeks before his passing away, when he had already lost the ability to speak. I asked him with tears in my eyes: "Dad, what can we do?" and he kind of shrugged his shoulders and I read in his eyes that he meant that he did not know, that there was probably not much we could do.

My dad who was so independent, self-sufficient, resourceful, able to do anything in this world and find a solution to any problem, had to let go. Not that he accepted it, he did fight all along as much as he could, against the nurses who would tie him to the bed, against the fate that was on him; he constantly repeated "it doesn't make sense", "it doesn't make sense", he was angry at what was happening; then he lost his speech, and little by little, day after day, I saw him go deeper and deeper in the silence of his illness, the thread to life becoming thinner and thinner until November 11, when he silently slipped in the invisible world. I received a phone call at night from the nurse who told me that it was over.

In the morning that followed, I went to see him. They prepared him on a table and let me in. It was surreal. I talked to him aloud for a long time; I wanted to touch him but I did not dare, afraid to be too close to the reality of the coldness of his skin. I wanted to keep him with me forever, I wanted to find the magic wand to get him back to life, but there was nothing I could do other than tell him how much I loved him, and I thanked him for being such a good father, and I wished him a restful time in heaven. Then I left. I sat on a bench outside, and I cried. I cried like I had never cried before.

Then it all started. I came back home to find that the brand new washing machine was acting weird, not responding to usual commands, as if all electrical connections were cross-wired. My mother told me that her alarm clock acted in a similar way, stopped working, then back on, but showing a completely wrong time or changing time while on, then the music started playing on its own. There was no doubt in my mind that it was my father showing that he was still around. He loved life and maybe these events reflected a last lost fight against an event he did not agree with, his departure, or maybe it was just to stay with us in a time when we needed him so much; we were all so distraught by his departure. As the strong head of the household, he knew that his passing would be a great loss for my mother and my brother who lived with them. He was the pillar of the house and it must have been difficult for him to accept that he had to leave because he knew that he was needed. I don't think I ever cried as much as that day. Losing my father was the most terrible event of my whole life. I had lost my father. The pain was indescribable.

But as I soon found out, I had not lost him, he was still around. Even though I could not hear his voice or hug him anymore, he had not left me. The signs he sent over the next few weeks after his passing were comforting; I knew he was there. Then they stopped.

About one year after his death, I was having lunch with a friend of mine and I told her how much I missed these signs. I talked about my father for a long time, with all my love and the strongest desire to be with him again. I was explaining to my friend how much I needed to feel the connection with him, how much I loved him and how much I felt his loss in my heart. It was comforting to talk with my friend about my dad and it made me feel better to share these very personal emotions with her. I drove back home feeling relaxed and when I opened the door, my daughter Caroline literally jumped out toward me.

She was completely out of her normal composure. "Oh My God, Mom! You have no idea what happened while you were gone! It was so scary! It was the loudest sound I have ever heard! Oh My God!" She could not stop saying that. She told me that while I was gone for lunch, all of a sudden the one-hundred-year old bronze statuesque alarm clock that belonged to my grand-parents loudly rang several times. This bronze alarm clock, which weights at least 50 pounds, was broken when I inherited it, so I could only remember the sound it had from childhood memories, when it stood in my grand-parents room and rang every fifteen minutes and counted the hours, when I would go and visit my grand-mother. Caroline was freaking out. She told me that the sound was extremely loud and intense, as these clocks can be. When she was finished telling me what had happened, I smiled at her and told her what it was. I felt so much peace. I knew that my dad was around and was acknowledging my call. It was his way of saying "I am here sweetie, don't worry. Just call me and I will always answer".

In the years that followed, he came to me many times, either during my sleep, in messages, or using again electrical appliances. Some of his visits were more intense than others. One of the most memorable was several years after his death, in the year 2000. I was listening to the radio and it played "What a Wonderful World" by Louis Armstrong who was my dad's favorite musician. I was alone in the house and I turned the radio louder, opened wide my arms, danced around smoothly, and said aloud with all my love, "this is for you daddy", and all of a sudden, the TV screen that was off started to screech and show interference lines. It was a wonderful way of telling me that he was around and that he had received my message of love.

I had a difficult time living only in the physical world and letting go of communicating with him. I read many books on the subject of communication with the other side, I read how electrical wavelengths are the closest to deceased spirits' wavelengths at night, when the brain is not as active as during the day, so I meditated and called my father every evening before I would go to bed. I knew that contact with the other side is not a light act and protection was required so that other undesired spirits would not stop by while opening the channel to your loved ones.

However one night, a scary episode occurred. As every evening, I had asked my father to come in my dreams and be with me, and I opened the channel I thought would welcome him. Then I fell asleep and then I woke up in the middle of the night: some beings were in the room and I felt an immense pressure on my legs that prevented me from moving. I knew I had to be more careful. I immediately sent them away, called for protection from God and loving spirits, and they left.

A few nights later, my dad came through. He told me "You need to live in the present and stop trying to contact us on the other side; this is not good. You need to live in the present; this is where you belong for now. I love you. Don't worry". Since I was always respectful of what my father said, I listened and stopped my evenings' attempts at opening the channels with the other side. The event that had occurred a few nights before had scared me enough that I decided to stop for a while and stay in the physical world.

Looking back at what I experienced then, I realize that I was trying too hard and went too fast without being prepared for it. The events that occurred to me several years later made me realize that we only progress as fast and as far as we can absorb and understand, like an onion that we peel, layer after layer, until you reach the core and then there is no layer left. As I experienced several times, some spirits are lost in transition and they take opportunities such as any open channel to come through. If not prepared to handle these lost spirits, it is very disconcerting for both them and the recipient of such visits. It was certainly scary enough for me that I decided to take a break from trying too much to get in touch with the other side. I was alive in the present for a reason and I had to move forward.

5

My Mom

If my dad was my hero, my mom was my passion. She was a lovely woman, always beautifully dressed with her hair and makeup done every day. It was important to her to always be pretty and well kept. She married my dad when she was nineteen, six months after they met at the 1950 New Year's Eve ball held in their hometown. Her cousin Jacqueline had told her how she had recently met a very handsome man who was a friend of another friend and how she had a crush on him. New Year's Eve was the perfect time to get together and celebrate. My parents fell in love right away and six months later, they were married. "I did not care about the white dress and the reception", my mother would tell us, "I just wanted to marry your father, so we just went and got married!" A photo of them taken the day of their wedding shows how happy they were to be together.

However life was hard for my mother. Her father had passed away when she was six years old and her loss always remained an open wound in her heart. She told us how she went to visit him at the hospital and that she was not allowed to kiss him because he had tuberculosis. She could only see him through a window. It broke her heart and she always cried when she told us about it. Her first son, my brother Joel, was born premature with dramatic health problems which would last all his life. When she gave birth in her house, she thought that his umbilical cord was very long but in fact it was not the umbilical cord. His intestines had developed outside of his body instead of inside. They had to rush him to the hospital to save him but he never fully recovered. At the age of fourteen, he almost died of an intestinal occlusion. After that, he stayed in the hospital for several months and he remained under medication for all his life. He was always a worry to my mother. Her second son, Dominique, was born two years later, in October of 1953. My mom always described him as "such a beautiful baby, with dark hair and dark eyes". He passed away on Christmas Eve of 1953, victim of an epidemic that killed many children.

Then in 1968, her mother passed away unexpectedly. At that time we lived four hours away and they did not get to see each other very often. So she was thrilled when family friends who lived nearby and were going to visit some family in my grand-mother's town offered to take her back to our house for several days. I was ten years old at that time but I still remember that day as if it were yesterday.

We were all excited to see her and my mother had cooked her favorite dish, a "pot-au-feu", a stew made of sausages, beef, cabbage, carrots, and potatoes, a very comforting and warm dish. It was almost noon, the house was filled with the delicious smell of a traditional dish that was the precursor of a good family time to come and we were waiting for their arrival any moment. I was playing with my sister and had a hard time containing my excitement. I remembered the last time my grand-mother had come to visit, she had taught me how to knit, and she told me a few things about life. I did not know her very much since I did not get to see her very often, but I loved seeing her and being around her. I would sit next to her on her bed when she was rewinding her green alarm clock in the evening. She also had a soft, small, dark burgundy leather wallet where she kept her coins and it had a very strong smell of leather. I don't recall any specific conversations, but I liked being next to her. She also always had some mint candies in her purse, as well as in her kitchen cupboard, which was the same color as her alarm clock! When I told her that I liked her alarm clock and her leather wallet, she told me that they would be mine the day she would pass away. She was funny, she always said that when she would die, she would want to be reincarnated as a cow because cows don't do much other than eating and sleeping.

So here we were, waiting for her to arrive. The table was set and we were almost ready. The only thing that was missing was fresh bread, so my mother then told me that she was running to the bakery to get some fresh bread and that we should tell our grand-mother that she would be back in a minute, should she arrive in the meantime. Then my mom left the apartment to get the bread.

A few minutes later, she was back upstairs. She was standing at the door, in tears, holding a blue piece of paper that she had just opened. At that time, there was no telephone and the only way to bring urgent news was by telegram. This is what she was holding in her hand, paralyzed with despair and sadness, the piece of paper almost falling off of her hand. The mailman had not bothered to take the elevator to bring the telegram to the apartment; instead he had simply glued a sticker on the mailbox that said "telegram". Finally, my mom read in tears the black letters printed on the white strips of the blue piece of paper which was this opened telegram. It said:

"Mother deceased".

My grand-mother had died in our friends' car soon after they had left her house. She had a heart attack, maybe too much emotion and excitement at the idea of coming to see us, at least that is what we thought.

So, yes, I can say that life was hard on my mother with the loss of several of her loved ones. However life went on and aside from these losses and the sorrow she had when she talked about them, she was a happy and outgoing person. She was also a loving mother who knew how to make me feel good. When I was sad, she was here to comfort me, when I was tired, she was here to help me with my children so that I could rest, and when I would wake up from a nap on Sunday afternoons, she always had a cup of tea ready for me and a piece of my favorite chocolate. And she smelled so good, her skin was as soft as velvet and I loved touching her hands, which she took great care of. "I would never go to bed without putting lotion on my hands" she would say, and indeed, every evening, after she removed her makeup, she would always finish her evening ritual by putting lotion on her hands that smelled like roses, and when she bent over to kiss me good night, I could smell the smell of her lotion mixed with the smell of her smooth skin. I loved her very much.

Then, in November 1996, my father passed away and with his death, my mother and my brother lost their strong pillar, their anchor, and they were adrift. The two years that followed his death were very rocky and difficult. I spent several months without seeing mom and when I finally went to see her, a tiny old woman opened the door. It was my mom. I felt so sad that day, so sad to have left her in her despair and loss at a time when she needed me the most. It was terrible. She was so happy to see me; so was I. Her skin was still as smooth as velvet and she still smelled her same soothing smell, but her face had many wrinkles from her sadness and solitude.

After a while talking, she told me about pain that she had in her mouth and I told her that I would take her to go to the dentist. A few weeks later, I took her to the dentist who immediately sent her to a specialist. A few tests later, she was diagnosed with mouth cancer. In March 1998, she was in the hospital for more tests and getting ready for surgery. At the same time, my brother who had been very sick for the past few months became worse. He could no longer walk, no longer eat, no longer function. His body was giving up. I had to take him to the general hospital to have him checked in. While mom was in a private hospital at one end of town for her surgery, my brother was in a different hospital at the other end of town. It was the same hospital where my father had spent his last weeks and it was hard for me to go there.

Once checked in, my brother let go very fast, within a few hours. He was resting in a private room and I went to see him. His body was cold like ice and he could barely talk. "Aren't you cold?" I asked him. "No" he said. He had already lost life, holding to the physical world by a tiny thread. I asked him if he wanted me to go and get mom. He mumbled with difficulty "if you want, little sis'" as he used to call me, so I took my car and went to get my mother out of the other hospital on the other side of town. I had to ask for authorization to get her out for a few hours; I filled out some paperwork, took her out of the hospital, drove back to the other end of town, and arrived late at night at the hospital where my brother was. We arrived in front of his room and the nurse asked us to wait a few minutes so that they would clean his bed.

She went in his room and was out within seconds. She walked toward us, looking at us, speechless; her look, fixed in my eyes as she was walking toward us, did not seem right as she stepped out of the room. She approached, one step at a time, like an automated, speechless robot. A few seconds that seemed an eternity. My brain was numb. I could feel something was wrong. Then she opened her mouth. "I am sorry" she said. Before she had time to move an inch, I jumped out of the chair, hoping that it was still not too late. But it was. He was gone.

We rushed in and he was there, laying on his bed; he had pulled out the oxygen tube from his nose probably in a last attempt at breathing his last breath, and he was no longer moving. My mom and I talked to him; I knew his spirit was still around, that he was not completely gone, and we both talked to him, my mom venting her frustrations of him being ill all his life and now leaving her, and me wishing him a good trip and rest. I felt sad to have missed him by a few minutes, I felt guilty that I had taken too long to drive from the other side of town to bring my mother to see him. I did not want him to breathe his last breath alone, yet, I had missed him by a few seconds. I was reliving in a few seconds the last hours that had gone by to see how I could have made things differently. Yet, there was nothing I could do. It was too late. No second shot at it. My brother was gone, and we were not next to him for his last breath. I was sad. Once again, I felt powerless. Death had won.

Then I brought my mother back to the hospital for her surgery that was scheduled for a few days later. Her surgery was a very long and dramatic one. I won't go into the details but I will only say that such suffering should not be allowed.

My husband and I had planned to move to the U.S. since we visited Montana in the summer of 1996. He was an American citizen and thanks to the sponsorship of his brother, we were able to apply for a green card for myself and the children. Our move was scheduled for April 1st 1998, two weeks after my brother passed away and my mother had her surgery. Our departure was directed by the imperative of the green cards. Once you have it, you need to leave your country of origin within a specific timeframe or you lose it. When we had decided to move, my mom and brother were still doing well. Things were quite different two years later.

On our way to the airport, I stopped by the hospital to tell my mother good-bye, but the intensity of the trauma had made her lose her mind. She was delusional and did not recognize anybody. It was a terrible moment for me. I think that I had gone through so much emotional trauma myself that some of my actions and reactions were robot-like, and I just had to move on. Maybe I was also subconsciously leaving behind that trauma, looking for a brighter and happier future. I was extremely exhausted by the pain and sorrow I had experienced these past two years. I told my mom good bye and I left. Once again, I did not turn around to look back; I had to go. I arrived at Sea-Tac airport in Seattle on April 1, 1998, as planned, and we settled there, starting a new life.

A few months later, my mother regained her sanity and my sister took her to live with her. It was a blessed time for both of them to be together and enjoy each other's company. And I was happy to know that my mother was well taken care of by my sister, surrounded with love and care. My mom seemed to get better but after a few months of chemotherapy and great suffering, her cancer made a rapid come back and she was given only a few weeks to live. I went to see her in October around my birthday, and she passed away two weeks later, in November 1998, two years after my father.

It was a very difficult and sad time for me. I was starting a new life in Seattle, which took a lot of energy, time, and effort to adapt. I missed a lot of things from my home country, but it was my choice and I had to deal with it; the trauma of having lost my parents and my brother was very heavy on me, and I cried many times. Months went by, my daughters were enrolled in school, I had found a job, and our new life seemed to be taking some sort of shape. However I often spoke about my parents, especially my mother, and I constantly thought about her. Little things that always remind you of your loved ones, a favorite dish, a song, or a proverb; my mom always had a song to sing that related to whatever she was saying or whatever was happening at that moment; and she always had a good old saying or proverb to apply to events of life, some of which were quite unique. She could be very funny. I missed her a lot. It seemed that I had no closure.

Then, on mother's day of 1999, she stopped by.

I was in my bedroom with my daughter Carolina and we were organizing the closet while talking about my mom. She had passed just six months before. It was Mother's Day, an even more special day when you no longer have your mom around and I was telling my daughter how I wished she were still around. Then, all of a sudden, Carolina and I looked at each other without a word, paralyzed in disbelief. The smell of my mother's perfume had suddenly filled the room. For maybe thirty seconds, her perfume was around us, very powerful. I asked Caroline "Can you smell it?" and she responded "Yes!" It was incredible. Thirty seconds later, the smell was gone. We smelled around the room, the pieces of clothes from the closet thinking that maybe there was a scarf that had belonged to my mother that would happen to be there, but nothing. The smell had left as suddenly as it had come. These few seconds were emotionally intense and my daughter and I were overwhelmed. It was as if for half a minute, my mother had joined in the conversation and the family moment we were sharing.

Then, more and more unusual events occurred.

As I said, my parents were very much part of our lives. For several years before we moved to the States, my parents and I lived close by in the same village, and we saw each other very often. So, of course, their loss was huge, especially since in a matter of two years both my parents and my brother had been lost. As we had settled in our new home in Seattle, we talked a lot about them. Until one day we realized that while they were not physically present in the room, they were listening, in particular my mother.

Each time we talked about her, the bulbs would flicker, and many times, ended up breaking. During meal times, each time we talked about her, the phone would make a weird noise, not a ringing sound but a very weird sound for one or two seconds, once or twice, and then stopped. It became so customary that we would joke about it and each time we talked about her, we expected the phone to ring or the bulbs to break. Sure enough, she was always responding.

One night, my daughter Elodie was in her room thinking about her and all of a sudden, the phone did the same again. This time, my mom had felt my daughter's thoughts and reacted to it, which was different from the usual times when we would talk out loud about her; this time, it was a telepathic response, a telepathic communication. I guess the phone was the best way for my mother to communicate as often as she wished, just a short way to say "hi, I hear you".

These communications had become so frequent that I felt compelled to research these phenomena. Until now, I had never researched the subject or tried to understand or investigate further communication with the world unseen. I was just receiving these messages as they came. But my mom's insistence and persistence led me to open that door. The perfume event was really the trigger since I had never heard of such a thing. I had no idea that spirits could use perfumes to show their presence. I wanted to find out more than the little I knew; I wanted to find an explanation to all the events that had already occurred. I wanted to open the door to the other side.

I felt that my mom wanted to communicate more, tell me more assertively that she was well and around. I now realize that it was probably my own need for her and the loss and sadness I felt about her departure that led her to contact me. Like when she was alive and I knew that a warm cup of tea and unconditional love would always be waiting for me, should I need any comfort. She was always here for me. And despite being on the other side, she still was.

After reading blogs and books that related to communication between this world and the other side, I found the name of a medium and I decided to contact her. I knew about mediums yet did not really know what to expect. But I thought that it was worth the try. If my mother was insisting so much, I thought that a medium might be a good channel for additional communication. At that time, I did not realize that I was a medium myself since I had been receiving communications from the other side for a while already. I guess I hoped for more. I hoped to hear my mother's voice again.

I was curious to see how the session with the medium would be since she was located in Utah and I was in the State of Washington, she spoke English and my mother spoke French; so I really did not know how she would manage to give me a reading with my mother from far away, on the phone, and in a foreign language, but I gave it a try. I emailed her and we made an appointment. I just told her that I wanted to contact my mother and I gave her the date of her death. Since my mother passed away in France, I was not worried about her getting any kind of information related to my mother as some people sometimes argue about mediums.

I feverishly waited for the time of the scheduled phone call. I was to call her at a specific time, so I prepared myself for this big event; I told my family not to interrupt me while I would be on that call, I went in a small room and got ready. I wanted to record the conversation, so I installed a small tape recorder, tested it a few times, and waited. It was my first time contacting a medium and I had no idea of what to expect. I was doubtful. After all, many people said that mediums were fake, that mediums used whatever information you said to create a conversation with your loved ones. So, while I was excited, I had also decided that I would not say a word that could discredit the medium's reading. I was not going to make it easy for her. At the time we had agreed upon, I dialed her number. A few seconds later, she was on the phone. A few words of greetings, she told me that the reading was starting.

At that moment, I tried putting the recorder on, but to no avail. I tried several times but it would not stay triggered. I gave up since I did not want to ruin the reading with this technical problem. I focused on what the medium was saying. At first, I thought that she was saying commonalities; my mom was happy that I had decided to contact her, she loved me, and the medium was saying other words that could come from anybody or even the medium herself. Then the tone of the voice changed. All of a sudden, the woman said something that only my mom would have said, with the exact same unique intonation that she used sometimes. At that moment, I let go of my suspicion and surrendered to the experience.

As if my mother were in the room next door, we started a conversation. She told me how when she arrived on the other side, she was greeted by her mother, her cousin Jacqueline and the son she had lost when he was three month old, Dominique, as well as my father and my brother Joel, who had passed away just a few months before my mom. She told me that she was glad she believed in Jesus because he was there as well. She told me about the beautiful house where she was now, and the garden, with amazing flowers that reminded her of roses. She told me very personal thoughts and how they looked after me and my sister from where they were, and that they could see our children, and that I should not be sad because they were well. As a note, my mother always spoke in the name of her and my father. She told me that they played cards, which was my parents' favorite activity, and other details of her life of peace and love. As if we were on the phone, directly talking to each other, we were talking again. She told me that she had the choice of her looks and had chosen to look like what she looked like when she was young and pretty, which was extremely important to my mother while alive; she would never leave the house without makeup, and getting old and wrinkly was definitely not something that she embraced.

We had been talking for about forty minutes when Sunni told me that it was time to end the reading. But as she had just said that, she added "wait, your father is now coming through; he wants to tell you something". It was a great happiness to know that they were together to talk to me and I was surprised, since my dad usually did not talk much on the phone. He told me that he loved me and that I should not be sad; he told me about his pipe, which I keep in a drawer of an oak cabinet that he had made from broken pieces; he also told me that he built furniture where he was, which was his main hobby while alive when he used to build miniature furniture. Thus, they were continuing their activities as when on earth. The tone of the conversation was very jovial and loving. I knew they were here, with me.

As my father finished talking and Sunni was about to end the session for a second time, she said "wait, someone else wants to talk with you, it is your brother Joel. Boy! Aren't they insisting, like pushing at the door all together to talk with you!"

My brother talked, calling me Little Sis', as he used to do, and telling me that he played music and that he was well. He told me that he would come and say hi and that I would know when it happened. But the most striking part of the conversation was when he asked for my forgiveness for when he was mean to me. It was incredible. He was indeed mean to me when he was eighteen and I was eleven. He called me the fat one and made fun of me in front of his friends. While such behavior can be typical in teenagers, it did hurt my feelings very much. As grown-ups, we never really talked about it and he was a very nice and caring person. He helped me many times when I needed help and he was a nice and sweet uncle to my daughters. Yet, from heaven, he was asking for my forgiveness for the only misdeed he had done while alive. It was very powerful and of course I told him that yes, I forgave him and I sent him all my love. I know he received it.

It was now an hour since we had started this session. We said good bye; I sent them my love and my thanks and we hung up. It was literally like hanging up from a phone conversation with my family who would have been on a faraway trip. I was transformed. I sat there on the floor of the room, still breathing their presence. With very personal details like the names of the people who greeted my mother, my father's pipe, and the name my brother used to call me, as well as the personal intonation of each of them coming through the medium, they proved their reality; with such vivid descriptions of their life in this new dimension, they showed me that they were alive in spirit and that they were happier than ever. Difficult to imagine spirits playing cards and having a beautiful house with flowers, but it is what it is.

There is no doubt in my mind that where we go after we leave our body is a beautiful, peaceful, and loving place where wonderful things await us. I knew they were happy and I was happy to have been able to communicate with them. It was a family reunion. I felt blessed and I was very thankful for this wonderful, extraordinary opportunity. I felt I had heard my mother's voice through the intonations she used during this conversation, through the medium, like when she was alive. It was also fascinating to see that earthly languages are not a communication barrier for the other side.

Since that day, my life hasn't been the same. A huge wall had fallen and in front of me was a vast, infinite landscape to be discovered. I had had a glimpse of the other side, at least I could imagine it from the conversation; I knew that my parents were looking after me and that their love went on. I learned that we are never left alone; we are never alone; we are always loved; even if we feel lonely, we should look for the hidden sunray that tells us that all is well; it is what I have learned from the many experiences I have had.

Communication still happens on a regular basis with my family. I know that it is part of life, and while some people might be disconcerted by such events, my children and I are comforted to know that my parents and my brother are still sharing family moments with us. Since that conversation, I have experienced many direct contacts with my family with no need for a medium. The channel of communication with them is wide open.

The last time such an event occurred was at the birth of my grand-daughter. My daughter was giving birth to her fourth daughter. Thirty years before, my mother had attended the birth of my daughter. This is the cycle of life, a beautiful one. I was standing in the corridor with my three other grand-daughters, waiting for the midwife's signal that we could enter the room; we knew that the baby had just been born. Finally we were allowed to get in and we excitedly entered the room. A beautiful baby girl named Ella Beatrice was born. We were all gathered in this room filled with joy and happiness. All was well, both the mother and the baby were doing well. Baby was already thirty minutes old and the nurses were busy taking care of her while my daughter was recovering from a hard labor. We were all very emotional, filled with the love and joy that such an event brings into people's hearts.

Then, all of a sudden, all the lights of the room flickered, and the electricity was off in the room. The nurses looked at each other, trying to find out what was going on, since this hospital is known for its preparedness in case of any major event, as all major hospitals in the Pacific Northwest are and where no power outage ever happens, but they could not find the reason for it. It went on and off for a few minutes, each time turning the electricity and all lights off in the room. You can imagine that at a moment such as right after birth, it is a concern for the nurses who are busy keeping the baby warm and taking the first health measurements. The first time it happened, we did not even pay attention to it since the natural light from the window was giving us some light and it lasted a few seconds only. Then the second time, it lasted about 30 seconds, and we saw the nurses getting nervous about it.

The third time, after it had again flickered and went on and off again, my daughter and I looked at each other, smiled and said: "the family is complete; they are showing us that they are around and that they are welcoming baby Ella". It was tender and magical to know that beyond their passing on the other side, they were still around, sharing precious family moments with us.

Beatrice Marx

6

The Love of My Life

As I described earlier, I lived happily in the family home, loved and cared for by my parents, until I left for college. We had great times together. They loved being social and having friends over and when I became old enough, I joined them in their outings, going bowling or gathering with friends. One day, out bowling with them, I met an acquaintance of theirs who was an engineer sent on an assignment from his home town in southern France to work on the construction of a terminal for super tankers next to Le Havre in northern France. Since he did not know anybody in the area, he soon became a very good friend of the family and started spending more time with us, sharing family dinners and gatherings with us. He was like part of the family. He was a very friendly, outgoing man and he was fun to be around.

After a few months, we felt attracted to each other and I fell deeply in love with him. He was older than me but the difference in age was not an issue. After one year dating, we were talking about getting married and he told me how he wanted to name our children. He was the only thing I wanted in my life. He was charming, loving, fun, positive, smart, educated, caring, and he made me feel like a woman. He had an adorable accent from the South of

France, the kind of accent that makes every word sing and be light. I was so madly in love with him!

I was still studying at that time and at the end of the school year, I missed an important test that was a step to enable me to be accepted in the next year of the program. Because I missed that step, I was told that I had to repeat a whole year of studies which I did not want to do. As a result, I decided to leave for England to study abroad for a year. I guess I was too young to realize the impact this decision could have on our relationship. He never told me not to go; he encouraged me to follow my path. So I left; I still see myself walking on the ferry to Southampton and not turning back because I knew that if I did, I would not leave. He was there, standing, watching me leave. What happened then turned my life around.

At that time we did not have cell phones or the internet; communication was mostly by letters. A few months after I had left, I came back home to visit and I found out then that he had made a woman pregnant and that he was going to marry her. I was devastated; the whole world was crumbling and life was not worth living any longer. I cried so much. But my love for him never left. He remained in my heart day and night through all the years of my life. I loved dreaming about him and us, even though I spent the mornings crying because he was not next to me. But life went on. I got married, then I divorced, but my heart still belonged to him. I saw him a few times after my divorce. By then he had divorced as well but he did not want to remarry or build anything any longer with a woman. It had been many years since our time together. I was happy however to see him in the neighborhood. I moved next to where he lived and a glimpse of him here and there was enough to make me happy. We were friends, but he knew how much I loved him and I knew he cared for me; he was always here for me when I needed his help, and I respected his decision not to be lovers again. He had two children with his wife, which he had named as he had told me he would when we were together.

Sometime later, I moved away and married for the second time. Years went by, I would still stop by and say hello since he lived by the beach and I would go there with my daughters. Then I left for the United States. He also moved away and I was never able to track him down and hear his voice again. My efforts in searching for him were fruitless; yet I still looked every day around street corners to see if he was there. He has always been a part of me, since the day I fell in love with him. There was not a day in my life that I did not think of him; not a street corner where I would not hope to see him appear. No matter where I was around the globe, I hoped to see him again. Years went by. I loved it when I dreamed of him at night, dreams where I was in his arms, where we were together. In 2010, I went to Maui with a friend and while driving, I saw a man on the side of the road who had his silhouette. My heart bounced, but of course in vain. It was not him.

Then, not long after my return, while I was lost in my thoughts during a lunch break looking through the window at the beautiful landscaped gardens and a few people having lunch sitting on the grass, came a banner in my forehead with the name of the medium I had contacted after all the events that had occurred after my mother had passed away. While I had completely forgotten the name of that woman, all of a sudden, her name appeared as a banner, in big letters, in my mind, erasing everything else I was looking at with my two eyes. My third eye was winning over the reality of the scene outside. As always when I receive such an insisting message, I have to follow up on it. I immediately researched the name of this person on line and soon found her phone number and email address. It had been more than ten years since I had contacted her for a communication with my mother and I was surprised that her name had showed up like this, out of the blue. Why would the name of this medium show up on this banner in big letters through my third eye when I was able to communicate directly with my loved ones on the other side?

I was very curious about it and decided to email this medium. I told her that I did not know exactly what to expect or who wanted to communicate, though I thought about my father since he had been the one who was communicating with me the most on a regular basis, so I told her that it was probably my dad who wanted to come through. I was not excited or impatient or expecting anything special. I just knew that I needed to contact her for a communication with the other side that, apparently, I was not able to initiate on my own. We scheduled a phone appointment for some time in the weeks that followed.

When the day came, I was excited. I was prepared to talk with my dad. I looked at memorabilia before the call, his pipe, which he had mentioned the last time we had spoken, his photos, and I was looking forward to talking with him. Then I called Sunni for the session. After the small talk that looked like general statements, it then became more personal and I was finally starting to feel the connection. I was taking notes while she was talking. And all of a sudden, she said: "Jean-Claude says hi". I stopped writing, my whole body was frozen, I lifted my head from the paper I was writing on and I said: "what did you just say"? She repeated what she had just said: "Jean-Claude says hi". "Do you know this person?" she asked.

I burst into tears. Jean-Claude is definitely not a common name in the U.S. and this woman was saying his name, the name of the man I have loved for forty years. I was able to respond between tears that yes, I knew him and that he was the love of my life. It was overwhelming. "Stop looking for me" he said, I am no longer there on earth, but I am waiting for you where I am now". It meant that he was on the other side, and that he knew that I was looking for him. The message of love that emanated from my heart was so strong that he could feel it even where he was. He was talking and I was crying. It was beyond anything I expected; I felt so close to him. "I always loved you" he said "and I regret that I did not marry you".

The love of my life, my soul mate, was the one who had called for this session. I was so sad to know that he had passed, but so happy to know that he was waiting for me on the other side. I had found him at last, and we would be one day reunited for eternity.

After the session, I had to find a way to confirm that indeed he had passed away. It was so surreal yet, so real at the same time. I had no idea where to look; who to call. Then I remembered the town where the mother of his children was from, and the name he had told me we would name our children when we were together. I rapidly investigated online, went from clue to clue until I found a phone number of someone who seemed to be his daughter: same name and home town of the mother. I gave it a try, hoping that it would be the right number. It was already late and with the difference in time between the U.S. and France, I knew that it was not a good time to call, but I could not wait until the next day. I was feverish with anxiety; somehow I felt it brought me closer to him.

The phone rang a few times, and I heard "Allo?" My heart was pounding. How could I say in a few words that I had just received a message from her dad from the other side who had told me that he was dead, and that I just wanted to have confirmation? Well, that is exactly what I did. The first response I heard was: "Do you realize what time it is?" I could not blame her. It was late indeed. And then "You believe in THAT?" and I responded "yes, I do". How could I tell her that it was not that I believed in it, but that I knew it as a fact? I could feel a lot of aggressiveness on the other side of the line, but I did not want her to hang up before telling me what I wanted to know. Her third sentence was "Anyway, what do you want?" and I said "I just want to know if your father is alive or not". And she answered "He died three years ago. And now I have to hang up. Call me tomorrow if you want." And she hung up. I was breathing heavily, lost in my thoughts that I would never see him at the corner of a street, sad that I was not next to him when he left for his ultimate journey, and blessed that he had contacted me from the other side to tell me that he loved me and was waiting for me where he was now.

I called his daughter again the next day, to apologize for my call the day before, and though she was brief on the phone, she did take my call and gave me a little bit of information on how he passed and when. I told her what her dad meant to me, I thanked her for taking my call, and hung up.

I am sad I was not able to hold his hand on his deathbed. But I know he is around, now and always. He is waiting for me on the other side, my soul mate, my love.

Real love stories never have endings.

The night that followed the reading, I had a dream, a message from the other side that was very symbolic and beautiful. There was a very bright, happy, colorful salamander, dancing around, having fun, filled with life and loved by all. Then it lost its colors, it became translucent and very quiet. At that point, I could feel that he was exhausted and that it was time for him to rest. He went away from the colorful, lively world, and slowly climbed up my shirt and nested himself in the upper left side pocket of my shirt, next to my heart, to rest.

In the morning, when I woke up and I turned the radio on, our song was playing.

Since that day, he has been communicating with me on a regular basis through telepathy, songs, and synchronistic events that bring us closer to each other.

Beatrice Marx

7

The Power of Dreams

According to what I have read during my research, sleep brings us closer to the spiritual world and creates a more favorable pathway to communication. Like when we want to listen to the radio and we turn the knob until we find the right frequency of the station we want to listen to, the reception from the other side is better if we are closer to their frequency. Spirits exist at a higher vibrational frequency and when we sleep, we also enter a higher vibrational frequency, which explains why spirits often communicate with us during our sleep. It is the time when our frequencies are at their closest.

As I explained earlier, all of my experiences in communication began before I was aware such things could happen, yet I knew that what was happening was not of the earthly plane. The same happened with communications that occurred during my sleep.

As I related earlier, my dad came through a few times during my sleep to give me messages. While they occur during my sleep, such visitations are very different from a dream. The encounter is extremely vivid. There is no background and no scene involved; there is only the face of the person that shows up as a snapshot and peace emanates from it, and there is nothing around the face of the person to blur the moment. Like when words appear in front of my forehead, or through my third eye, to give me a direct, short, yet unavoidable message in the form of a banner, these visitations take up all the space available in the screen where it is being played.

During the day, there are always multiple thoughts taking up our brain, constantly going from one place to the next. During dreams, the same happens. Many actors, places, objects, actions, exchanges of conversation, emotions, sometimes crazy scenes that seem to be nonsense take place. But in the case of spiritual communication, telepathy happens one word at a time; the message is concise, clear, and powerful. The image appears as a single picture and stays in my mind long enough to remain imprinted. Nothing around it to disturb it or lose it among other images; only one snapshot. When I wake up, I know that I received a message as it is the first thing that comes to my mind when I open my eyes.

When my father contacted me during my sleep, his face appeared to me, very clear and alive, and he looked straight at me. Through telepathy, he conveyed his messages, from third eye to third eye I would say. Like a laser going from point A to point B. No words are verbally spoken, all happens in telepathy, but in a very strong and clear, vivid tone. Words are then imprinted in my mind, until I wake up.

Recently, I was thinking about my mother, about how much I loved her and how I wished she were still around; I wished she could see my home, my children and grand-children, and thinking how nice it would be if she could stop by and chat. I even asked her to make something move in my living room to show me that she was around, hoping that she would use her maybe now available magic powers to show her presence, but nothing moved. I also thought that maybe I should leave her in peace, as she was probably having a good time in her new home. Anyhow, it was a moment like we all have, when we think about our loved ones who left and we wish they were still here physically. So after a short while, I wished her good night and went to bed.

When I woke up, I remembered immediately a message that I received during the night in the form of a few words, the same kind of message that had happened to me a few times during the day while I was awake. Words appear like a banner in the middle of my forehead, big huge letters that take over the whole space of my thoughts, coming out of the blue, totally not related to the thoughts I am having in that specific moment, and not always making sense.

That morning when I woke up, the first thought that came to my mind were the words "Jade Pleure". These words did not mean anything to me other than "Jade is crying" or the words "Jade" and "tears" in French. As I said earlier, when I receive a message, I know that I have to investigate until I understand its meaning. It is an empowering thought, like a huge box in front of me which I know I have to open, no matter what. I have no clue, but I need to find the clue because I know, deep inside, that it is a message from the other side that requires further attention. I just know. These messages do not leave my mind until I do something about it. So, that morning, as soon as I was out of bed, I went on the internet and typed the words "Jade Pleure". To my surprise, something came up immediately; it was the title of a song and the name of its singer who was from the West Indies. I found the lyrics and read them. And I understood. My mom had answered my request.

My mother had used inspiration from her favorite place on earth, the West Indies, where she had some of the best times of her life while on vacation with my father, and Zook music, the music from Guadeloupe and Martinique, which she also loved, to send me her message. It so happened that *Pleurs* which means *Tears* is the title of a Zook song, sung by a singer named *Jade*. When I read the lyrics, I cried, but this time, thankful and filled with joy to know that my mother was around. Here is what the lyrics say:

> Car j'ai autour de moi
> L'amour de ceux qui m'aiment
> Ils sont loin et pourtant
> Je les aime autant
> Oui, j'ai autour de moi
> Et ce malgré la distance
> Le soutien de ma mère éternellement
> présent

Which means:
> I have around me
> The love of those who love me
> They are faraway
> But I love them as much as they love me
> Yes, I have around me,
> And this, in spite of the distance
> The support of my mother eternally present

You can imagine how I felt while reading these lyrics. My mother, beyond the physical world, had used a song from her favorite place while alive to send me her comforting message. It is difficult to explain how it can happen and I do not try to explain such event. It is beyond the explainable and comes from a world beyond the world we know; it simply proves that there are no boundaries between the physical world and the spiritual world; everything is possible. The connecting thread is strong and everlasting. The power of love is eternal.

What was really amazing in this message is that she used the lyrics of a song from 2006, a time posterior to her death, and from Guadeloupe, her favorite place on earth, to send me her comforting message. Maybe this is where she spends her time now, in her favorite place on earth!

Wherever she is, I know that she will always be here for me when I need her support. No need to call her, she is around, no matter what.

Such messages from loved ones are available to all. It just requires we be open to this reality with all our heart, and ask for a sign. Spirits are very resourceful and they are eager to show us their love. They know what signs to send us so that we make no mistake and recognize their presence.

Beatrice Marx

8

Messages from the Other Side

After twenty years of receiving messages of love from spirits of people I knew and loved, one day I started receiving messages from unknown spirits that I had to transmit to other people. I had become a messenger. Initially, it was quite surprising and I did not know what to do with such messages, but it soon became clear that I had become a medium of communication between the other side and our physical world.

A few years ago, a disagreement and misunderstanding lead my friend and me to lose contact for about a year. Then, all of a sudden, her name came to my mind unexpectedly; it also came up on the internet, or during conversations with people, or during other synchronistic events. Day after day, week after week, it seemed that I was urged to contact her. And one day came a clear message to me: I had to contact her and tell her "don't do it". I had no idea what that meant, but the message was so clear and insistent that after a few days, I had no other alternative than calling her and telling her. Finally I emailed her and asked her if we could get together for coffee.

I was really happy to see her again and after some casual conversation, I told her about the message. Again, it was difficult and awkward for me to convey such a message, but it was like a mission: I was the conveyor of an important message and I had to deliver it. I have learned since then that this is indeed how it happens. I don't try to figure out the meaning of the message or whether I should or should not give the information. I just do it. The recipients know the context and it all makes sense to them. It is not up to me to understand.

When I gave her the message, it immediately made sense to her. I will not divulge the explanation since this was a personal matter, but it didn't take her more than two seconds to understand the message. From beyond, her son was looking after her. It not only helped her with the specific matter this message was related to, but it also helped her heal and know that her son was and would always be around.

It is not always easy to relay such information but I would not deceive a spirit by not conveying whatever message they entrust me with.

Spirits can be very stubborn and tenacious. They don't let go until you acknowledge them.

One day I received a message from Jean-Claude, the love of my life who told me himself about his passing. His message was clear. It was an emotional message that does not require words to convey. I could feel his sadness and limbo state when he asked me to tell his daughter that he loved her, and that he asked for her forgiveness. Like my brother had done before, again I had a request for forgiveness coming from the other side. It confirms that closure is needed in order to reach peace; not only on earth, but in the next realm as well. In the case of Jean-Claude's message, I not only received the message, but I could also feel a deep emotion in this message. I could feel his deep love for his daughter as well as his deep sadness for whatever misunderstandings they experienced in their relationship during his lifetime. I do not have any information about it and it is none of my business. As a transmitter, my role is only to convey the message to the third party. When I receive such messages, I cannot go on with my daily activities until I act on them. It is like a post-it note always hanging in front of my eyes. So, after a few days of persistent request from the other side, I called his daughter. I knew it would be awkward since the last time I had talked with her it had not been a very positive experience. She did not believe in the other side or spirits, so I had to prepare myself to give a short, concise, and right to the point message. I felt the obligation to convey the message I had received and I knew that the sender of the message was eager to know that I had conveyed it.

So I called her. As I expected, she was not very friendly, but I politely told her that I had received a message from her father and that I had to give it to her; I did not want her to hang up before I could deliver the message, so I was fast. In three sentences, I gave her the message and told her that I had nothing to add to it; she told me that what happened between her and her dad was none of my business, and she was right, and I certainly had nothing to do with it, except that I was given a mission by her father that I could not ignore; I had to give her these two simple yet so powerful messages that her dad, from the other side, wanted to make sure she would know. I said good bye and I hung up. I just hope that she opened the door to her dad if it was closed since this is what he felt from where he is now. This is what spirits wish for when they initiate such communication. They also need closure.

My guess is that spirits are happy to find a thread of connection between their world and ours to convey messages that are important both to them and to the receivers. I once went to a presentation by John Edwards, famous medium that spirits love since he helps them communicate with their loved ones on earth, and he was explaining how many spirits were waiting to be able to communicate with people who were attending his session. In the case of Jean-Claude's message to his daughter, I literally felt like a mailman; no personal emotion was geared toward me; it was all about his daughter and I could really feel his strong love for her and sadness related to the situation between them.

It also confirmed the importance of forgiveness beyond the physical world, so that peace can fully be reached, and lessons fully learned, until only love and peace remain.

Not long ago, I had the opportunity to receive a different kind of message from an unknown spirit. This message was aimed at making right a wrong situation that had occurred during the lifetime of the spirit; it proves that any wrong deed should find justice, no matter how long it has been since the deed had occurred. It seems that requests for forgiveness are as important to spirits as requests for justice.

I live next to a small town famous for having several ghosts living in its Victorian houses. The town organizes ghosts' tours on a regular basis and it requires signing up at least two months in advance to be able to participate in one of these tours. The guide explains where the ghosts live, and with the help of a ghost meter or EMF sensor, he calls the ghosts and communicates with them. While our tour was not successful in getting any verbal response from ghosts through that night, we ended the visit in a house that is famous for its extensive and regular paranormal activity. I was taking many pictures, hoping to find some spirits' auras on the pictures when I would download them back home. I was not paying much attention to what the guide was saying as I was going from room to room in this large Victorian house. The only thing I knew was that in the 1880s, a family lived there with children and a maid.

Up on the third floor, as I entered the nanny's room, I could immediately visualize her room as it was when she lived there, where her furniture was, where she hung her clothes, and sat to read and think, and I could feel her emotions. I looked through the window, watched the night sky outside, and while it was a dry day, I saw rain drops falling along the windows. A lot of sadness was emanating from this room. I took some pictures, left the room and walked toward the tour guide. Before I knew it I was telling him: "the woman who lived in this room was raped by the owner of this house". The guide, surprised, looked at me and responded "actually, not by the owner, but by a friend of the owner, but I don't want to talk about it".

I was surprised by his response, yet did not insist since it was a tour group and I did not want to create any disruption, but I knew from the message I had received and the strength with which I said those words that they were sent to me by the woman who used to work for this man. It was not me talking, it was this woman taking the opportunity of my presence and probably feeling the compassion I felt for her when I felt her sadness to convey her message through me. And the message was clear: she was not raped by a friend of the owner, but by the owner himself. How can we find justice on past events? I think it is important to bring peace and closure to people who suffered and could not have the truth be known.

    This woman, because of her status, could not fight for her rights, and this man, because of his status, would not be held responsible for the misdeed he had committed; the official version then became that it was a friend of the owner who was responsible. I sent healing thoughts to this woman so that she would know that someone cared and that she was not alone; it was the best I could do. I can only imagine how she felt all her life not being able to tell the truth, and having to live in a world of lies.

    Though where she is now, I am sure that she is surrounded by a lot of love, I felt that sending her genuine loving thoughts from the place where she was still lingering in search of justice might bring a little bit of comfort to her. The guide told us that a child was born from this rape and problems eventually occurred that lead her son to be confined to the basement where he still remains, haunting it. I did obtain several pictures with large auras from that room. I hope he also finds peace.

    So, yes, I do think that sending healing thoughts makes a difference, not only with spirits, but around us, in our daily lives. When words cannot be heard, sending healing thoughts and love can make all the difference.

9

The Angel of Love

So, until now, I had seen and heard ghosts. I had witnessed their ability to create interference in objects, and I had received many messages. I knew that their love was always around me and it was very comforting. Yet, one day, I experienced the most overwhelming visitation one can imagine. It was a Saturday afternoon and I was feeling lonely, which rarely happens since I am more of a lone wolf than a social person. Yet, that day, I missed the presence and the love of those I loved who are now gone. I felt it would have been nice that day to be all together and share a family moment as we used to have in the past. I felt alone.

I was laying on the couch of my living room, facing the window pane that opened onto huge evergreen trees. The sun was slightly coming through and I enjoyed the rays of light flickering from the movement of the leaves on the trees outside that were reflecting in my living room. I soon fell asleep, rocked by the movement of flickering light and the silence of that afternoon. After a while, I woke up. I opened my eyes. Next to me was an angel of light, like a translucent floating veil.

It all happened very fast. I felt this angel hugging me with his wings of floating bright, translucent white light, bathed with the most pure and intense love I have ever felt. There is no word to describe it. I felt like a baby, pure of any thought, completely surrendered to the love, care and protection of his mother. Yet the level of love I felt from the embrace of this angel was beyond any human love you can experience. It was intrinsically felt in the core of my being, soul and body. It was as if I was part of this angel when he took me in his wings. My body was still on the couch, but my "true self", my eternal spirit, was with him. It was an out of body experience where I deeply felt oneness with him, oneness with a Universe of love bigger than what we can fathom. I was completely, entirely wrapped and bathed in love and peace. It was extremely intense in beauty, yet so smooth, silent, and peaceful.

And I heard telepathically: "You are loved and you are not alone. All is well. Remember, you are loved".

It was the most powerful feeling I have ever experienced. I wanted to stay there, held in his wings, bathed in his love, but it only lasted a few seconds. I felt comforted and I felt the unconditional love of this angel for me; as if I was everything to him; as if I was under his entire protection and care. Then he left.

I thought "if this is what is on the other side, then I know what paradise is: LOVE". A love without any condition, explanation, thought, worry, time, and essentially all that makes our physical world sometimes heavy. Love from the other side, as I felt it from the embrace of this angel is a pure, crystalline, light, with an intense feeling of wellbeing all over, the feeling that nothing can ever make you sad or fearful, that you are loved and protected, no matter what. Negative feelings do not exist in divine love.

It was overwhelming, completely wrapping me, taking me to another dimension; it was not merely a vibration of love, but a complete wrapping, in and out, of infinite, unconditional, pure bliss and love. It is difficult to describe because it does not belong to our physical world, but it is comforting to know that those we love who left are surrounded by this eternal, pure, whole, and divine love, and that one day, we will join them in this divine, loving world.

Beatrice Marx

10

The Power of Love

People who pass on to the other side remain in our heart with all the memories we have about them, but they go on to a new life as spirit; they go back home, where they came from. We, humans, are embodied spirits, and our bodies are a tool to make us go through experiences to improve our soul, until we learn everything we have to learn which is basically that all that matters is love. Yet we have to go through a multitude of various experiences until we get it; lifetime after lifetime, until we finally understand it, until we breathe it, until we are one with God and His word; that all that matters is Love.

My brother's request for forgiveness during our supernatural phone family reunion made me understand how important our actions on earth are. I realized that we are accountable for all our actions and thoughts and that none should be left in the red. The awareness of what love means is what we are here to learn, and it is not easy. Many situations test us during our life time and I think we reach peace once love becomes natural and constant in our thoughts and ways. Not only do we reach peace within, but we also get closer to God, to the core of the universe, to the golden ball of unconditional divine love. It is not a process of a one-minute thought. It takes time to understand, assimilate, and put in action. As I said earlier, we go at our own pace and only receive as much information as we can handle before going up to the next level of awareness.

As I was one day in contemplation, admiring a beautiful sunset at a remote place in the Caribbean, I started talking with a man who also seemed to be soaking in this divine beauty. We both shared comments on the beauty of the place and he asked me what had brought me there. I told him that I was writing a book.

As he asked me what my book was about, I started telling him about it. I told him my book related the contacts and messages with my family and other spirits from the other side; I told him what the other side seemed to be, based on these communications, a world of love and peace where we all go, free of baggage; and I told him about the episode of my brother asking for forgiveness, how important it was for those who passed to know that they did not leave any negative feelings behind; that their souls on earth were here to learn love and whatever had not been done in love had to be examined and repaired in some way, so that their soul would go up in higher spheres, closer to God and to the concept of unconditional love for everything. He was very receptive and we discussed these ideas further.

Then, he asked me "how can you ask for forgiveness to people who have already passed away?" He went on telling me of an instance in his life when he realized later that he had hurt people, which he did not mean to do at that time, and I could feel how heavy this guilt seemed to be weighing on him, and that he wished he could repair any hurt feelings he might have caused. While he was saying how much he wanted to ask for forgiveness to those people who had passed, but did not know how to do it, I could feel the energy of his message literally leaving his aura and going directly to the recipients who were receiving it. It was beautiful and very emotional; it was more than vibrations of love, it was like strong, golden, ethereal rays of love emanating from him and going up in the universe. And I answered to him: "You just did it!"

What matters is to truly feel the message we want to convey. We can ask for forgiveness to anybody who passed away, thus finding peace within, by simply asking for forgiveness, with all the genuine love and sincerity that can only come from the heart.

The same as we can ask for forgiveness, we must also be able to forgive, starting with ourselves. We are humans and we are not perfect. We should always remember that and be gentle with ourselves. Once we forgive ourselves for our imperfections and actions we can regret, then we can start loving ourselves. Then we are ready to forgive the others, and ask for forgiveness. And we do not have to wait to be on the other side to do it; we need to let go of our pride and ego and ask for forgiveness while we are on earth.

Pure love, divine love that comes from the heart is all it takes. It is not easy to forgive and ask for forgiveness since it requires letting go of the ego and become humble, but by trying, we realize how rewarding it actually is, and once we reach this level of love and peace within, we feel a wellbeing that we can then spread around. If words are too difficult initially, just an aura of genuine positive thoughts can make a difference. This is the effect of Divine Love in our heart. The difficult part is to become aware of our ego and pride and its effect around us, and decide to let go, little by little, so as to restore more balance in our life and interactions. Then, the Divine takes over and helps us go further.

As I was talking with that man, we started discussing the unhappiness and sadness so many experience, while we were both feeling so much appreciation for this moment, facing the sea and looking at the sunset, breathing in the peace that was emanating from it all. He told me that back home, he was surrounded by people who were old and sour in the assisted living place where he was now living, and how these people were waiting for their last breath, without any hope or positive thought in their mind or heart, sour about their lost ones, sour about their upcoming death, which they could not wait to arrive soon enough, yet which they feared because of the unknown it represented. He said that it was sad to see everyone feeling down and that they were expecting him to feel that way as well. It was unnerving to these old people to see this man happy and enjoying the gift of life while he had lost his wife eighteen months before.

While he was trying to explain to them that he was not feeling sad through the grieving process because he knew that his wife was still around, people took him for a lunatic, or a man who was in denial; they all expected him to fall apart at some point. We talked about what to do in such instances, when we are surrounded with people who have negative energy and who are so locked within themselves that no word can reach them. It is a fact that we cannot change people, we cannot change the way they think, act or react. Yet, we can still make a difference.

When words are useless and will not be heard, we can always send thoughts of love, spreading them from our golden, or silver, or white aura, whatever is the way we represent our own ball of divine light and love, and spread it outward toward those who suffer from sourness and sadness. It is again an energy work, a state of being, that can make a difference in our everyday interactions. We all feel the bad and draining vibrations that emanate from negative people. We do not know what other people go through and we cannot help them directly in their journey because each of us has to go through our own experiences and lessons to advance further in the development of our soul.

Yet, we can still be of help by sending vibrations of love toward these people, wishing them well and peace. We do not have to interfere with their lives, emotions, or experiences, just sending them genuine love and wishing them well can make a huge difference. They do not even have to know about it, but we should not be surprised when we see a difference in their behavior, as a heavy weight is lifted and positive vibrations get through to them. The key is to remain uninvolved, yet send them genuine feelings of love, send them that sparkle of love that comes to us from the divine, which they still do not see or feel, or do not want to see or feel. It does require an effort on our part: that we take the time to stop and pay attention, that we hear what is being said or not said, and that we acknowledge these people's feelings.

Namaste: "the divine in me honors the divine in you". We can all be conveyors of divine love. Genuinely send vibrations of love toward those who cross our path knowing that these vibrations of love come from higher spheres going through us to help each other and the universe.

One day, start smiling at everybody who crosses your path and you will see the effect of divine love. All of a sudden, people's eyes lighten up, dark or lifeless emotions of the face are replaced by a sparkle in the eye, muscles of the face relax, and positive vibrations are timidly emanating from it all.

Surreptitiously, you are making a difference in the Universe.

11

The Purpose of Communication

The messages I received from the world unseen since I was a little girl evolved in content, mediums, and purposes, and came from various sources, angels, spirit guides, loved ones who left before us, God, the Universe, and other beings from another dimension. Peace, love, and harmony are a constant feature in these communications.

In order for the universe to be balanced and healthy, it requires that embodied spirits on earth as well as spirits of those who departed feel at peace within. Interestingly, more and more communications with the non-terrestrial world have been occurring over the past ten or twenty years, and it seems that since the beginning of the twenty first century, people are more open to the concept of another dimension and the reality of a spiritual world. Or maybe it is because more and more people are open to these parallel worlds that more communication occurs. There is also so much material available today to open the channel of communication with the other side that the wall between both worlds is becoming thinner. While it was often considered taboo forty years ago, there is a great need for such connections nowadays, and I feel that the need comes from both sides. It seems that the fear of the unknown made, and still makes some people closed off to such communication. Some consider that people who pass away are dead and gone forever. However, only the body is gone. The spirit is not. Spirits in fact exist before birth, they are incarnated when they are born, then they lose their carnal envelope at the time of the death, but the soul still exists. They are impalpable entities as we know it in our physical world, but they exist; they are energies. What scares people is the stigma attached to ghosts, spirits as featured in horror stories, and the warnings from the Church against ghosts and spirits. Yet, they are energy as much as we are as embodied spirits, which explains kinetic and electrical interferences. It seems understandable that they would be able to play with electrical appliances to make us know that they are around since they are direct energy themselves.

Yet, we should also be aware that some spirits are lost and might play tricks that are not always enjoyable. They have not transitioned yet and they are still in between layers of different dimensions, staying at lower frequency levels, thus closer to the earthly plane. These spirits need help to get going, so that they understand that they are no longer supposed to be here and that they now belong to the other side. It seems that when lost spirits are helped in the process of leaving the earthly plane, they seem to be happy to go, rather than staying in limbo. They might be stuck where they died, like the ghosts who died on the highway in Spain and who still did not know that they were dead. Tales we hear about scary ghosts do exist and should not be dismissed. Some ghosts linger at a lower frequency level and vibrate negative energy, which requires people who try to contact spirits to use care and respect in their endeavor, since these spirits are to be avoided. It is important to always vibrate positive, high energy before opening oneself to the other side and address the spiritual world with love. It ensures that only spiritual beings of light will respond.

Not long ago, I was walking in the small town where I live and something, I do not know what in particular other than a leading force, led me to the local cemetery, a historical cemetery where only people from the 19th and early 20th centuries are buried. I never go there and I did not have any particular reason to go, yet, my feet took me there. It is certainly a gorgeous place with a beautiful view over the Hood Canal, in the Puget Sound, and it was an enjoyable walk, though it was almost dark, and cold. As soon as I reached the cemetery, I saw two young teenagers and from the way they walked around the cemetery, I could feel that they were trying to communicate with spirits. It was right after Christmas and they probably had received for Christmas the brand new equipment that they were using. I walked toward them and showed interest in what they were doing; I asked them questions while looking at their recording machine. One of them thought that he had just heard a sound through his earphone from his highly sensitive equipment while walking next to a tomb. So I asked them if they had done such investigations in the past and they responded that it was in fact their first time.

This village is a very haunted place. It is still as it was in the 19th century and I suppose that the former inhabitants of the place like it enough that some never left or were never kicked out by the extremely negative interference that heavily populated areas can create. So, anyway, we talked a little and I told them about the town and its ghosts. I also gave them a few suggestions on how to approach spirits, and to always respect them, never force our presence upon them, always ask for permission to be around their places, and always thank them for letting us be around. I felt again that day the connection between all realms. And I knew that it was not a random personal decision to go to the cemetery. I was sent there by the Universe to bring a little bit of information to these unprepared teenagers who were entering an unknown world like jumping in the middle of the ocean without knowing what was underneath.

Contacts go both ways. While we contact spirits mostly for emotional comfort and to reactivate the thread of life and love between them and us, spirits contact us for various reasons.

They might have unfinished business, like this nanny who was raped and who, from beyond her grave, wanted the truth to be known. They also show up simply to say thank you, like my grand-mother who stopped by my mother's bed at night.

Spirits also need comfort. They need to know that we love them, and that we forgive them for whatever harm they hold themselves responsible for toward us, like my brother who asked for forgiveness. Any unfinished matter needs to be resolved and real closure is needed for both parties, the one who stays and the one who left. And most importantly they want us to be happy. They want to help us heal. Time is not an issue for them. They will stick around as long as needed. My mother and my father show it all the time.

Ask and it will be given to you, seek and you will find, knock and the door will be opened to you. These words from Matthew resonate when I think about the spiritual world because they are the essence of a peaceful, loving existence. Trust in the universe and you will never lack of anything, certainly not of love. We just need to learn how to receive, and then, give back, unconditionally. The ripple effect of love and peace on a large scale is a reality that we need to grasp and put into action.

My gradual experience with the world of spirits led me to study, be open, investigate, research, and the more I learned, the more I was open and the more communication I received. We only receive information as much as we can absorb and accept. Spirits do not want to scare us. Spirits are eager to communicate if we only give them the chance and the medium to do so. If the channel is not open, communication won't happen. It is like a telephone line that is not plugged in.

However, if we are open to it, it will happen. Not every minute of the day, but whenever we open the communication channel, or when spirits feel the urge to communicate an important message. Then they will try everything until you open the communication channel and acknowledge receipt of the message. Like a phone that rings and you have to answer. No questioning, no trying to understand, we must just accept it as a fact, our communication between this side and the other side is real. Sometimes, the messages are clear, and sometimes, more subtle. As we accept as a fact the existence of spirits on the other side, they show up more easily. As I said, they do not want to scare us and they will not show up unless they feel we are open to it. Once they know that we are not scared and that we are open to communication, they use familiar signs to show their presence. They stop by during our sleep to help us deal with earthly matters. We can even converse with them. Events, words and thoughts are to be acknowledged. They are no coincidences. When we ask for communication, we are able to create the connection with the other side, all of us.

Spirits love us, the beloved wives, husbands, mothers, fathers and children that they left behind; their major concern is our happiness. They also want to protect us. Of course we still have our free will and we can decide whether to follow their advice or not. However, the few times when I was contacted by spirits in such instances and I relayed the message to the recipient, it made total sense.

The purpose of divine communication is to bring messages of love. Love as we know it usually refers to a very restricted, narrow realm; mostly our family, friends, pets, etc. Yet, this love can be further expanded. Love heals. We need to learn how to heal ourselves as individuals, resolve our trauma that we carry from lifetime to lifetime, find peace within, and then expand towards the outside. As long as we carry trauma and unfinished business, we cannot think about the wellbeing of the earth or its inhabitants because we are too self-centered around our own personal problems and trauma. Many people lack trust in the Universe, always afraid of tomorrow, of the what ifs, of the yes but, and think that they are holding onto their survival in the shape of a paycheck to pay for their mortgage and electronics, with the fear of losing their jobs, hence access to all these materialistic items that poison our world. Once we solve our own traumas and unfinished business from past lives and past events in our current life, we can then open up our aura of wellbeing and communicate it to those who need it. The love we receive from the other side is meant to help us heal so that we can heal each other and heal the earth.

I know that I could not have written this book a few years ago; I had to go through all the lessons I was here for, I had to shed my share of tears and reached a clean slate to be able to be where I am today. As I said earlier, lessons and teachings happen one at a time, at our own individual pace. We cannot force that pace. When I look back at my life, I feel that each event was a lesson to be learned that led me to the next level, like in a video game, where you need to go through obstacles before you are allowed to go to the next level. I have always felt very connected to the other side, and I went through many lessons, some of them were extremely hard, but I learned from them. I would not be where I am today if I had not gone through these lessons. And today, I feel blessed; I look back and I thank all those who were part of my life for the lessons they taught me, the love or hurt that came from these encounters, and the strength I gained from it all.

There is so much sadness on earth that if those who feel peace and love within could send out vibrations of love to all who cross their path, the ripple effect would expand these positive vibrations around, and as a result, more people would feel the peace that divine love brings.

I sometimes think, "God, I wish I had known thirty years ago what I know today" but I could not have. There is no fast forward in life. We need to enjoy every single moment, every minute, live in the present, listen, look, learn. There is a lesson to learn in every encounter we make, in every experience we live.

When I was young, I lived more often as a victim than as a person in charge of my own reality. I was in survival mode and went through all kinds of traumas. My only focus was raising my children, having a job to feed them, and be healthy to raise them. I loved them dearly and they were my only concern. How can you think of the wellbeing of your surroundings when you are hungry, unemployed or abused? While we do have to go through all the experiences, bad or good, that life brings us since they are part of the lessons to be learned, we should always remain hopeful and trustful in the universe. We are not alone and we are loved.

If we believe and have faith, and if we are genuine with our requests, we receive the help we need. God, the Universe, spirits, guides, angels, they are here for us. I do think that their main concern is our happiness and wellbeing.

If we are happy, we convey positive energy which in turn has a ripple effect and multiply the positive energy around us, benefiting not only our own health and happiness and the ones of the people that we meet daily, but also our environment.

Times have changed. We no longer have to belong to an organized religion to be close to the source of love. The new spiritual age has now come where more people become aware of their oneness with the universe. More people are now channeling these messages of hope and love that come from the other side.

A new paradigm is emerging where people are embracing their responsibility for the peace and love they wish for. We have the power to change the world for the better.

Forty years ago, if you burnt some incense, had long hair, went to Katmandu and praised love and peace, you were considered a hippie, a utopist, or an unrealistic person who maybe was smoking too much pot. Today, New Age stores are everywhere, and we, who believe in the possibility of peace and love, are no longer considered hippies. Yet, of course, in terms of numbers, we are still not many, but with the power of love and the ripple effect of positive energies and positive thinking, we can make the difference and spread the word. The teachings of the masters are no longer kept in secret societies or by organizations that control the masses; they are now directly available to millions of us through messages, direct communication, and openness to the other side, bringing us awareness to the reality of a universe bigger than what the eye can see.

Beatrice Marx

PART TWO

ETHEREAL MESSAGES FOR THE GOOD OF THE UNIVERSE

Beatrice Marx

12

Visions and Predictions

After all my experiences with the spirits of loved ones, and as my research on the topic started to give me more answers and open up my awareness on the infinite world outside of my own little world of mundane activities, I soon discovered that in addition to spirits of loved ones, there was also a whole realm of spiritual beings out there that were waiting for me to be ready to receive messages of another level. Guardian angels, spirit guides, and other beings from a fourth dimension soon came through and opened a whole new world to me, like I could have never been able to fathom. One day, I realized that the level of communication had shifted. It seemed that I was ready for more. Now that I knew of the divine love, and that I understood Its power, I was to expand It beyond the physical and spiritual world to the earth itself. I was to be shown the healing power of love.

As I said earlier, we only receive information up to what we can assimilate and understand. Our teachers show up one after the other at the pace of our learning. All the help I found, all the resources I ran into, all the people I met showed up at the right time in my learning process. I never had access to a source of information before I had assimilated the former one and was ready for the next one. Like a six-hundred page instruction book, I had to go through chapter after chapter before getting to the end, when I would finally be ready. At the time of my learning and quest, I certainly did not know where it was all going, where I was going, I only knew that one step had to lead me to a next one; I did not question anything; everything just came naturally.

So, one day, after all the personal messages I had received, which I just related, messages of a different dimension started to be conveyed to me. The messages expanded and I started receiving messages and information about events related to the earth that were about to occur. They came through in the form of physical discomfort, as well as codes, words, very clear and unmistakable messages. Initially, I did not know that they were related to future earth events, yet because of their repeating pattern, I soon felt that they were not randomly occurring. They were linked to a new reality: I was now physically connected to the earth.

I realized that I could predict a volcano about to erupt. By the pressure I felt in my head and especially my ears, I knew that the earth was about to express herself. The pressure was so unbearable that my head felt like the volcano containing its fumes and magna about to erupt but waiting for the cap to open up. The first two times it happened, the pain was so intense that I went to see a doctor. The doctor diligently looked in my ears and saw pressure on my eardrums, yet he could not tell me why I was having such pressure since I had no other symptoms. Each time he told me to use eardrops and come back if I was not feeling better. Each time, 24 hours later, a big volcano erupted. I started writing down my physical symptoms since they were coming out of the blue, were very strong and painful, too much to be ignored, and each time followed by an earth event within 24 to 48 hours, after which time my symptoms disappeared.

The first one, I remember, was in Indonesia; then several followed. May 21, 2011, I woke up in the middle of the night with intense, painful ear pressure. At 5:30pm local time (9:30am Seattle time) that afternoon, the Grímsvötn volcano erupted in Iceland.[3]

After I had identified the pattern related to the volcanos and the relationship between my symptoms and the eruptions, similar patterns occurred before big earthquakes would happen. On October 20, 2011, I had huge ear pressure in both ears and a headache. On October 23, 2011, a 7.1 earthquake occurred in Turkey[4]. August 4, 2012, intense pain and ear pressure; August 6, 2012, 11pm, Mount Togariro erupts in New Zealand[5]. August 9, 2012, intense pain and so much pressure in my ears that I felt my eardrums would break open. August 11, 2012, earthquake in Iran[6], 180 dead. So it seemed that the intensity of the pain was on a par with the intensity of the event.

On and on, without fail, I could feel the earth's next movement. As if my headaches and earaches reflected the pain that the earth was going through, I could feel her malaise before it hit. The big earthquakes usually announced themselves by huge headaches, not the ones that are throbbing, like a stick on a large drum that would hit it every second, but the kind that takes your head between a press and squeezes it, accompanied with intense non-stop pain, usually on one side of the head; it could be the left, the right, the top, or the bottom. I wondered if my head was like the earth, showing the location of a future event through the location of my headaches. I ended up finding somewhat of a pattern, not as specific as being able to tell the country, but I could say in what part of the globe the events were about to occur. Sure enough, 24 hours later, the earthquake occurred.

I can still predict such events since the same symptoms still occur. When it all began, these occurrences left me helpless. I also received geographical information through letters that were imprinted in my forehead. April 9, 2011, the word SAMO appeared. Samo is an Italian city near Messina that was devastated by an earthquake followed by an undersea landslide in 1908 which caused casualties amounting to between 100,000 and 200,000 dead. That same day, Mount Etna, the Italian volcano located close to Messina in Sicily, was in intense activity.

I also received many messages of various kinds related to destruction by water: major destruction of huge territories by water to come in the future. One of the most overwhelming messages I received was in April 2011 when the Mississippi river flooded. I received the exact location of where it was to start and its path all the way down to the Gulf of Mexico. I received images and words that reflected future destruction of land by water. I drew it on a map and sure enough, a few days later, it happened. It was overwhelming.

Why did I receive such information? What was I supposed to do with it? I knew that there was a purpose other than impressing my friends with the fact that I could predict dramatic events related to the earth. I thought about calling towns to let them know but they would have thought I was a lunatic. Can you imagine me calling the mayor and say: "Good morning, Sir, I just wanted to let you know that you need to prepare your town for the worst flood ever"? So, I was left with a list of events that I had received information about, and confirmation of the event when it occurred a few hours or days later.

I was desperately looking for help. It had been going on for several months now, and I really needed help figuring out what was happening; I needed to find out what to do with this kind of information. Furthermore, I felt I was in an awkward situation because it was not the kind of things I could discuss with any random person. They would most likely think that I was crazy, or they wouldn't be of any help.

The only thing I could do at this point was to record in my notebook the messages I received and the corresponding events that occurred soon after. I hoped that it all would make sense at some point.

Beatrice Marx

13

Planetary Healer

While these communications occurred, I still had to live a normal life and go to work. As a few months had passed by peacefully, busy in my normal routine, problems of a different kind started to occur.

For several days in a row, I had experienced problems with my computer, especially with the key board and the mouse. On and off, the connection would stop between the hard drive and the peripheral components and I had to reboot the system, turn my computer off, wait and see, and try again. As we all know, it can be very frustrating to be stuck in the middle of a task because your computer is not responding. After a few days of these occurrences, I asked the IT guy at the office to come and help me. He tried to trouble shoot the problems but was not able to find what was wrong. After checking everything he could think of to solve the problem, he told me that he could not figure out what was wrong and that the USB plugs had probably died. He gave me a new keyboard, a new mouse, and a new hard drive, but on and on I would get stuck with unresponsive devices. A second new hard drive later, the IT guy was puzzled, he had never seen that before and he could not explain what was happening.

Not only were the electronic devices over charged, but I was too. I could feel a surge in energy through my body as if I were plugged onto 220 volts. I could feel the energy flowing through my whole body, limbs, organs, chest, heart; it was very uncomfortable and physically overwhelming. I started realizing that maybe I had something to do with the electronic and electric breakdowns. I decided to try and remove the energy from my hands before touching my desk and computer. I am not talking about static effect here, but of real electrical energy going up and down my limbs and my whole body. I tried grounding myself, and sending this energy out of my hands. Despite my efforts, it happened again. The calculator had now joined the computer, screen and other electronic devices. As soon as I touched an electric or electronic device, it seemed that I was creating a short-circuit and the devices stopped functioning.

At home, I had similar problems with my computers and the internet. After several days of frustration, calls to the provider for help and nobody able to find what was wrong, I decided to have fiber optic installed in my house since I was told it was very efficient and reliable and would solve my problems. Yet, a few days after it was installed, I ran again into the same problem of unexplainable breaks in connection. Once again, I was faced with a puzzling mystery that technicians could not explain.

Finally, after about a month and a half of electric and electronic disturbances, normality came back to my technological world. But my body was still experiencing these interferences. It is easy to make the connections after the fact, but when my dis-comfort started, I really felt that something was wrong with me. Very uncomfortable with these physical feelings, I scheduled an appointment with my regular doctor who sent me to see a neurologist.

I called to schedule an appointment with the neurologist and was told that the first available time was five weeks away. By that time, my legs and arms were really bothering me a lot; I dreaded going to bed at night since as soon as I laid down, my legs and my arms were as if pressurized, and I could not stay in one place. The pressure and the current inside me were so intense that I felt sometimes that my whole body was squeezed and wired. The energy needed to be released, but I had no clue how to do it. I couldn't fall asleep until after my exhaustion had finally won the fight. I tried everything I could think of to relieve the pressure and the compressed trapped energy. I would hit my legs and arms, massage them, pinch them, walk, drink milk and eat carbs in the hope of falling asleep tired by digestion, nothing was helping. I looked on the internet and googled my symptoms. I thought I had multiple sclerosis or fibromyalgia, or one of the lengthy unknown diseases that are listed when you enter three words of symptoms on Google.

When I finally met the neurologist for the first time, I was looking for immediate help as I was exhausted from the symptoms. I went through a lengthy questionnaire and more tests including an MRI of the brain. All came back normal and I was desperate for an explanation and a name on my dis-ease. Tests after tests, I realized that my health was good and that there had to be another explanation for it.

While discussing it with my co-worker, she mentioned that maybe it was related to a past event when maybe I had received an electrical shock. I looked back in my life and remembered that indeed I had received an electrical shock twice in my life; the first one was on an electrical fence in Normandy while crossing the fence to go and see cows when I was young. The second time was in Spain, when I received a 220V shock from the electrical cord of a lamp while trying to unplug it. However, I felt good and confident that the electrical shocks I was experiencing now were not related to these events that had occurred more than thirty years ago. My guess at that point was that the source of the problem was beyond the normal, beyond the world of traditional medicine and explainable phenomena. I asked my friend if she knew of anyone who could help me; she was very resourceful and I hoped she would know someone who would understand what was happening to me. Sure enough, she knew of a woman whom she thought might be able to help me.

Her name was Penelope.

I looked on line to find out who this person was and I read all the information that was available on her website. She described herself as a mystic and clairvoyant "dedicated to the well-being of this planet and all those who live here", and as a planetary healer. I was dying for help and was willing to explore any resource in depth. I found on her website information she had posted on "Reconnection" and checked the link she offered to Dr. Eric Pearl's website[7]. I read it, hoping to find answers to my quest. The information I read was compelling enough that I decided to buy the book he had written. As I said earlier, I was willing to explore any avenue, read as many books as possible, meet as many people as possible if they could offer me whatever help they had to offer. I read it in a few hours. I found similarities between his experience and mine. His first realization that something out of the norm was happening, the messages he received telling him to continue doing what he was doing, the energy he felt, the feeling that what he was doing was conveying something from the other side, that he did not control it but was only a conduit. And I realized that maybe the root of my problem was to catalyze the energy I felt in my body into a healing energy. I felt less alone in my journey and could start to see some meaning in my physical symptoms.

Meanwhile, I met with Penelope, in desperate hope that she could help me. Our meeting was scheduled in a New Age book store, and the atmosphere was very soothing. I waited there for a few minutes, browsing around the store. She then came toward me and greeted me. I could feel peace emanating from her and I immediately felt at ease with her. She led me to a small room where a soothing light was lit and two chairs were facing each other. Though I thought I would start my conversation by telling her about the physical trouble I was experiencing and the intense energy I felt in my limbs, and that I hoped she could help me, I just went on and on describing how I felt spiritually, how I felt I was on the verge of a major shift and that I did not know what to do with all of it, the messages I was getting from the other side, the predictions I had received about the earth, and the urge to move forward.

She listened to the long description of my experiences, encounters, messages, and plea for help, and then she said: "Welcome to my world! You are a planetary healer!"

Here I was, starting to understand that the energy I felt in my body was not useless and especially that I was not the only one to experience such energy, my body shivering with excitement from the realization that I had finally found answers that made sense and felt like natural reality. I realized that the energy I felt in my body was a tool that I could use to heal and communicate.

Heal the earth, heal people, and bring out love and peace in people so that as a ripple effect, the community of healed people would heal the earth. This is certainly difficult to fathom and comprehend for people who have never experienced any of this but for me, it was a relief. I could finally see what I was supposed to do with all this. It was really difficult for me when I received the information related to the flooding in the Midwest back in April and I did not know what to do with it. Penelope basically explained that there are planetary healers all over the planet in this new era of planetary consciousness and if we all sent healing thoughts to the earth, we could cover the grid of the earth and help it go through this change with less damage. I did some more research and found out that indeed I was not alone, there were more and more people like me and that we are stronger if we unite our forces to help the earth heal.

My knowledge about healers was limited to what I had heard as a child, which awoke in me a very strong curiosity since they were known to be able to heal people's ailments just by merely touching people or bringing their hands close to people's body. I remember going to one when I was a child, and later, as an adult, for a sciatica. They are known by word of mouth and highly respected for their powers. I never questioned where their powers were coming from, and I never thought that such powers could be used for higher purposes. To my surprise, I discovered that healers are active practitioners of wellbeing recovery all over the world, not only for people, but also for the earth.

Messages such as the ones I receive are neither new nor rare. There have been many messages from the spiritual world since Antiquity. What is new is the commonality of such messages and of people's ability to heal. People are more open to it, thus receive more tools to use these abilities. Instead of individuals located in remote villages and acting on people's sciatica, they are now gathering in communities and joining their healing prayers for the good of humanity. Whether the recipients of such messages say that they come from extra-terrestrial entities, angels, or spirits, they all leave a very strong imprint in those who receive them. These messages are spiritual teachings for us to act upon. I discovered that some organizations organize "prayers marathons", where people all over the world at specific times join to say from their heart and soul healing prayers for the earth and the Universe. It seems that it has become of the utmost importance to the Universe that we become aware of our power and our impact on healing the world, and that we understand that the only way to bring peace to the earth and the Universe is to channel and to breathe this divine love, until all loving spirits become one.

So, as I left Penelope and understood better what was going on, I started working on catalyzing the electrical energy I received in my hands, like a student with a new tool and manual. It was quite fascinating to feel the ball of energy going from hand to hand. I also meditated a lot to receive more help and answers from my guides since it was all new and I needed guidance on this new path. But I felt a huge weight had been lifted. Through a whole maze of unknown, I had finally found the door to a new world for me. I felt so relieved and light. I knew what direction to go now. I felt really blessed and thankful for all the resources and help I had found on my way and I took the time to assimilate all the information I had recently received about what to do with such energy and what it meant to be a planetary healer. I also noticed that my physical symptoms were alleviated when I worked more on catalyzing the energy and releasing it.

Then, I saw the manifestation of what sending love thoughts and healing wishes could do.

One day, my coworker brought her dog at the office, a very old dog, peaceful and almost ready to go from age. The poor, old dog looked at me with her tired eyes, barely moving her head from the ground where she was resting. I petted her, consciously opened to receiving love energy from above and releasing it onto the dog telepathically; simply sending words and thoughts of love toward her; while her head did not move an inch, she immediately responded with a weird sound and her mouth twisted in a weird fashion up on one side. My friend saw it and exclaimed "Well, what is that? She has never done that before!" It reminded me of some of Dr. Pearl's descriptions of how patients reacted to this receiving of healing energy and it seemed that the physical reaction of her dog proved that she had received my message. It was comforting to have a direct proof of energetic communication; no need for language, emotions were going through telepathically and energetically.

What was really important to me in this instance was the fact that the dog had acknowledged my message of love. Telepathic vibrations of love had gone through. And I realized how important thoughts could be, positive thoughts, and how they could bring peace.

Positive and loving thoughts are available to all of us; they do not require any special training or skill. It is what emanates from our aura while we walk, live, talk and interact with others. The more positive vibrations we feel and send, the more positive and loving our surroundings and those in it will be, and with the ripple effect, maybe indeed we can expand peace in people's hearts and heal the earth. Sometimes, the most obvious things are the ones that take us the most time to realize. Love in our daily interactions, genuinely felt and conveyed, could literally change the world, by bringing peace and feelings of wellbeing to those who receive such love. No need for words, just genuine thoughts of love.

Beatrice Marx

14

Heal the Water

So, all these events that had happened to me since I was eleven were maybe meant to open my awareness to the other side, to the fact that we are all connected, past, present, future, the known and the unknown, and that we can heal ourselves, each other, and the earth all together. I certainly discovered that there is more in life than what the eye can see. My horizons expanded toward an infinite, open world, where we are all connected. By now, I was not only aware of a world beyond the physical world as we know it, I also felt one with the Universe.

After receiving messages from the other side on events to occur for quite a long time, they stopped. I asked my spiritual messenger if there was anything I should know. He answered: "We will tell you; you will know; you are ready now". So with this information in hand, I just went on with my life, until the next message. Many months went by without receiving any messages, and then, all of sudden, a new message showed up.

One day, as I was connecting with the universe, during those moments of peace and connection that respond to invitations I receive from beyond, a vision came to me, a visitation with a very strong message. Three beautiful Naiads with very long hair were sitting in a grotto, next to an almost dried out source of water, and they were sad. I immediately felt an ethereal connection with them from beyond the world I know. All three were looking at me. They did not move; they just had their eyes connected to mine. I could feel the intensity of the moment. As I looked at them, I felt part of them. No words were spoken. All occurred through telepathy.

They told me that they needed my help, that it was an agreement we had from before I was incarnated and that I had accepted to be sent on earth to help heal the earth, especially the water. It was a very powerful encounter; I knew that these beautiful women were related to me from beyond the earthly plane. They were my "Sisters of the Stream". I could feel their deep sadness and the urgency of their request, the need for help beyond their realm. And I could see the desolation that was to come on earth from the almost depleted source of water in the grotto. Sparse drops were falling from the top of the grotto like tears of sadness from the dramatic situation related to water on earth, representing the scarcity of water and the critical situation it was in. As always, the intensity of the feelings that go through such moments is beyond words. Through connected thoughts, they conveyed it all.

Interestingly, I have always been attracted to water; I always need to live near the water; and a few years ago, while talking with a friend who was asking me what was important to me, I told her that, while it might seem a shallow interest, I was really into rivers and I loved being on my kayak, floating down rivers and that I felt I was home when I was on the river, that I felt I was part of it. I had the opportunity to run the Colorado River in the Grand Canyon for two weeks a few years ago, and every day was a day of magic. I felt I was at home, back to my source. I did not know at that time how much I was right. But each time I leave the river, I cry, as if I am leaving behind my beloved. My strong emotional connection to water and the messages I had received from my Sisters of the Stream as a planetary healer led me to do more research on how to effectively help in the healing process.

While I knew the destiny of water on earth was not on my shoulders alone, I knew that I could contribute and I had to find more tools to do so. While researching the subject of healing of the environment, I found out about Dr. Emoto's experiment on water, which was fascinating.

Dr. Masaru Emoto[8]'s experiment on the effect of words on water shows how we can have an influence on our world. He proved with photos how thoughts and feelings can affect reality. He poured water in various glasses to which he repeated either nice, loving words, or bad, violent words. He even went further with writing such words and taping them on the glasses. Then the water was frozen and he analyzed the crystals of the frozen water. The water that had received negative words and thoughts created murky, twisted crystals, while the water that had received positive energy gave beautiful, symmetrical crystals that resembled snowflakes.

As my Sisters from the Stream had told and showed me, the world is suffering from human abuse and water in particular is becoming very scarce and polluted. The result is more dramatic than what has even been imagined by scientists and humans. Lakes dry out all over the globe, rivers are fishless and oceans are polluted. And it is only going to get worse. Yet, it seems that the scientific world has not been able to reverse much of the human abuse that has been destroying it for the past century and a half.

Dr. Emoto's experiment helped me understand that I had actually in my hands the tools to help in the healing process. All this energy I received that made me unable to control a laptop without breaking it, I could use it in a different way. Once I realized what it was, where it was coming from, and to what effect, I was able to understand how I could help.

I started meditating more and more, asking for guidance and divine love. I tried to learn how to get to the source of healing; if my sisters wanted me to help heal water, I needed to learn how to do it. I learned more how to catalyze my energy and started using it. As I related earlier about my friend's dog, I had noticed how powerful thoughts of love could be. I started developing more and more this concept, and use it around me. Sending my love through my energized hands and my thoughts to whatever was around me, the trees around my house, the bay and its clams and oysters, the people I met randomly; I started sending love telepathically to all that came across my way.

The more I did it, the more I felt connected to the divine love and to the infinite thread that connects everything from this world and the other. I knew that I received messages and was connected to the other side for a reason of a bigger purpose, but I needed to find out how I could be of help. I knew I was getting there.

Yet, normal daily life and its multitude of activities sometimes distracted me and I sometimes forgot to work with the energy that I received until it was too much to handle. Energy must flow, and while I was receiving it, I was not letting it flow. I felt electrically charged and this surge in energy I wasn't releasing was making my daily life very uncomfortable. Probably a way to remind me not to forget to use this energy for a beneficial purpose!

While on a trip, I made an appointment for a massage to help release tension and electricity in my body; of course, as always when I have needed it, the perfect person appeared on my path. The lady who was to give me a massage was from the Island of Mauritius. After about thirty minutes into the massage, she asked me questions of an ethereal nature. She had felt in my body this surge of energy and the source of it. She said: "You cannot keep this energy in you, you have to release it. You have to use it to heal your surroundings, whatever calls you. I am a healer, and I know what you are going through. You were given this gift of healing and you have to use it".

She helped me, gave me new tools, and reminded me that it was my duty to serve the Universe. She told me about her own experiences, and how she catalyzed this energy to heal people; she told me how she received the healing energy from Higher spheres and how she was able to heal fevers and illnesses. And she told me that I had to seriously start releasing the energy I was receiving; that I had been given healing powers to use them, and that if I felt an overcharge in my body, it was because it was time for me to release and send out this energy.

The next morning, before sunrise, I was out on the beach, and followed the suggestions she had given me. Bathed in the beauty of nature, I grounded my feet deep in the earth, and sent the energy I had received from the golden beam of light and love of the Universe toward the sea. Within seconds, I felt I was inside a huge ball of golden light, bright and sparkling, and from this light in which I was standing, I could see and feel thousands of beams of light all around me going toward the sea. It was extremely powerful. All a sudden, I felt I was in the middle of the ocean, not my body, but my spirit, swimming with the fish, feeling the movement of the waves under the water and seeing each invisible particle of the sea. It was magical and powerful. I was part of it; part of the ocean and all of its creatures. This out of body experience was peaceful, magical, pure in silence, and harmonious, extremely harmonious. It felt like a dance of all creatures together in perfect harmony, and I was among them.

As I said earlier, I always meet teachers when I need them, at the right time and moment. This woman was a healer herself, and she told me how she handled her energy to heal people. Thanks to this woman, I was back on track.

15

We are all Divine

One morning, I knew that the day had come for me to take on a new adventure. I had learned the lessons I was supposed to learn and I was ready for more. Bigger projects were awaiting me, dreams, a mission, and my destiny, all of it at the same time. When I decided to follow the impetus for this great move, I realized that it was just the normal next step to take on my journey. While it seemed like a huge decision, it felt simple and easy. There was no other alternative, and I knew there would be no turning back, I knew all would be well. Of course, I thought about the practical impacts of this huge decision, as any responsible person would, yet, I felt at peace with that decision.

So I told my supervisor at work that I was resigning. I knew that my life in the corporate world was about to end and that a new, amazing, wonderful life was awaiting me. I knew what I wanted to do next, yet, I did not have everything planned out, all the details set up ahead of me, which was very unusual for me, since I am a born planner and organizer. I knew that I was in good hands, in the hands of the Universe. I was ready and willing to take on whatever next would come my way.

As it is polite and customary to do, I sent an email to all staff in the department where I was working to let them know of my departure, saying that it was time for me to follow my heart, that it was time for me to write the next chapter of my life before I would get too old to do so, that I had many rivers to run, many quilts to create, and many stories to write, and that I was going on a new adventure of life.

Within hours, I received the most amazing and unexpected responses to my email. I would come across people in the elevator, or at the coffee machine and they would all tell me how I was an inspiration to them. Some even emailed me to let me know how my email had made them ponder their priorities in life. And to those who wished they could do the same, I told them: "Well, you too can do it". And the response was invariably the same: "Well, I can't do it; the mortgage, the loans, etc." And I realized that indeed, what I was about to do seemed to many an impossible dream, a craziness, or a great leap of faith, something that most people would never, ever dare to do. As far as I was concerned, there was no question about it; I knew I was in good hands; I trusted the universe, I knew I was doing the right thing at the right time, and I felt it was my destiny.

I feared nothing; not that I was reckless, or irresponsible; I just knew that I would be well taken care of. An ineluctable, delightful destiny was awaiting me.

I realized that many people were functioning under the authority of fear and that they could never be fully at peace while living under fear. It is amazing how I felt the day I set up my intentions, without any "yes but", or "what if" to cloud them, and I fully trusted the Universe, knowing that all my needs would be met, and that I did not have to worry. If I had kept the fear of ghosts for their potential malevolency, I would have never been able to receive all the supportive messages I have received. I would not have been able to catch the thread of connection between the earthly world and the world unseen, though it is where answers to the world's current sickness are to be found, where our future resides and our eternal bliss awaits. If I had been afraid of tomorrow, I would not have resigned from my job to go where I knew I was called.

Many people stay in their current living situation for fear of the unknown. And if we sent a poll to people who work, I am sure that we would get at least 80% of unhappy people because they hate their jobs, yet they wake up every morning to go to a job they hate, until they retire, and the unhappiness they feel all their lives create diseases in their body that end up killing them when they finally retire. If they only forgot about their fear, and jumped into the life of their dream, they would be happy, spread their happiness around, and make a difference all around. Nothing is impossible. We just have to trust.

Yet, you might ask me, who should I trust? Well, the Universe, and God. I do not want to appear proselytizing here, but the love I have been talking about, the love that comes from higher spheres, is the love from God. This has nothing to do with organized religions that appropriated themselves the idea of God and gave to Him all kinds of bad attributes to make people fear Him.

When Jesus came on earth, it was to spread the notion of Love among people, not to set up a restrictive, fear inducing organization under the cover of what was soon to be called the Christian Church. Again, fear was part of organized religions because the main purpose of religion was to put order in societies and keep societies under the yoke of governments.

The Bible was not the first book to set up rules that condemned wrongdoings. In any society, civil rules are needed to create order and prevent anarchy. Hammurabi[9] (1795-1759 BC) preceded the Bible with his code of laws. Some even say that Moses copied some of Hammurabi's laws three hundred years later. Murder, theft, adultery, false testimonies, coveting the neighbor's assets, all bad deeds condemned by Hammurabi that we also find in the Bible. Hammurabi used his secular laws "to make justice visible in the land, to destroy the wicked person and the evil-doer, that the strong might not injure the weak"[10]. The Bible uses the same laws through the fear of God.

Does it mean that all good deeds that people would do under the rule of the church would be done, not from the heart, with pure and genuine feelings of love, but for fear of God? How can we be one with God if we fear him? How can we really feel love and convey it if we only follow the principles of the Bible for fear of God's judgment? It should be the opposite. Since we are in the image of God, as everything around us is, and we are, as everything around us is, divine, then we should love every living being as we love ourselves. No fear of God, only naturally positive, loving thoughts for the sake of it, with, as a bonus, the ripple effect of divine love. Right now, I think that people should fear the consequences of their own negative actions; God has nothing to do with it. Humans are the ones who have been bringing on the global situation of war and destruction upon themselves. Yet, they can reverse it, if they want. We are in charge of our own reality and we need to take responsibility for our life, our environment and each of our actions, reactions, and thoughts. Remember the ripple effect!

When Jesus came on earth, he merely wanted to let people know about God's love and about the fact that we could all reach peace within if we only followed his precepts of love. Unfortunately, history has proven that men of love who try to convey the message that we are all one and that we should love each other do not last long. They are a threat to authority, and need to be eliminated. Again, I do not belong to any organized church. I know that God is, and that Jesus existed, just like Muhammad and Buddha and other prophets. And they all came with the same message of love.

My research for answers led me to a book called "Messages; Communications from the Spirit World" received by the Medium James Edward Padgett 1914-1920, Love is the Heart and Soul of the Universe" (Joseph Babinsky, James E. Padgett)[11].James Padgett was a medium who received messages from various spirits between 1914 and 1920. Some came from family members and friends, others from Jesus and a few of his disciples. The messages from Jesus are simple and clear. Divine Love is the solution. If we want it, we will receive it and we will find peace and full happiness.

One of his messages received on September 24, 1914 and addressed to James Padgett said:

> "I am a son of God as you are. Do not let the teachings of men lead you to worship me as a God. I am not. The trinity is a mistake of the writers of the bible. There is

no trinity; there is only one God, the Father. He is one and alone. I am His teacher of truth; the Holy Spirit is His messenger and dispenser of Love to mankind. We are only His instruments in bringing man to a union with Him. I am not the equal of my Father; He is the only true God. I came from the Spirit world to earth and took the form of man, but I did not become a God – only the son of my Father. You also lived as a spirit in that kingdom, and took the form of man merely as a son of your Father. You are the same as I am, except to spiritual development, and you may become as greatly developed as me".

He ends one of his other messages with the words: "I love you with a love that will never end" (message from January 13, 1915).

He also says "This Divine Love is also the influence which makes men on earth think and do that which makes for peace and goodwill among men. It is not possessed by all men, in fact, by comparatively few, yet its influence is felt over nearly the whole earth."

With these words, we are far from the fearful God the Bible and the Church have used to control societies, and the last message confirms the effect of Divine Love: "while not many have it, the influence is felt over nearly the whole earth". It gives us an idea of how the whole earth would feel if more people were open to it.

It is time for a new awakening and for acknowledging a spiritual reality aside from any organized religion. It is time for the realization that we are all part of a collective consciousness beyond the precepts and dogma of churches and that we all have the power to make positive changes among humanity and our environment. It is time that people on earth realize that we are all after one same ideal: peace and love, and that the word of God is the same in whatever religion: Love.

No need for any organized religion or prophet; we are part of the Divine and we can all bring the message of love onto earth. It is not a surprise that more and more people have become messengers of the Love of God. The new paradigm that was predicted by many called for a world of love where individualism would be replaced by a community of loving minds.

While it is said that Jesus will come back, and the Jews are still waiting for their prophet, I think it is time we realize that while Jesus was a messenger and the son of God, so are we the children of God, thus part of the Divine, and we are all His messengers. So, instead of Jesus coming back, or any one new prophet, we are all being given the possibility of spreading the teachings of Love as Jesus did it two thousand years ago. Instead of one Son of God spreading the word of God, which is Love, we now have millions of us, Children of God, spreading the same teaching, millions of us acting on the teaching of God.

We do not need a new prophet since we already know the message. It is too easy to rely on outside sources as the source of a solution when we have had it all along in us. We can now visualize how millions of us spreading and living Divine Love can affect the world, not only human beings, as I said earlier, but the earth, the environment, all living beings. Furthermore, in addition to the good this Divine Love does to the earth and its inhabitants, it raises the level of our higher selves, our spiritual self.

Living in Divine Love would dispel all negative thoughts, war, greed, jealousy, disrespect. We would all act in pure, genuine love toward each other, and our spirits would be elevated to make one with God, through his teaching of Love. It is quite simple actually: we all get rid of negative thoughts, ask for Love in our hearts, once we have it, we feel so much peace and happiness that we spread it around, and as a ripple effect, we expand peace and love around. Then, we realize that power, greed, love of money, individualism, and everything that is responsible for a lot of negative effect on earth and people would disappear on its own.

This is definitely one of the main purposes of communication with the other side: that we can be messengers of love and spread that message, not only in words, but mostly in actions and reactions, which would all become based on love and respect. The forgiveness my brother asked for was related to a lack of respect that had a huge impact on how I felt about myself later on. The power of words! As my mother used to tell me, "turn your tongue seven times in your mouth before you speak".

All the messages I received from the other side, these direct communications with the spirits of those I love who crossed over, were all related to love; on and on, these spirits told me about their love and their wish for us to be happy. They do not want us to be sad. They showed me their presence with all these electrical interferences I related earlier because they knew I was sad and I needed their support; this is why they came through, to answer my call for love. They want positive energy to surround us and be with us.

We, as embodied spirits, human beings living together on this earth, need to remember these messages. We do not have to wait to be on the other side to ask for forgiveness or forgive, to act with love and kindness every day of our life, to respect everything and everybody, not for fear of consequences, but with a feeling of goodness, always remembering the ripple effect factor.

There are more and more messengers of love all over the earth; many without even knowing it. A touch of grace one feels all of a sudden while looking at a peaceful sunset, while welcoming a child when he leaves his mother's womb to start his earthly life, when a child tells his mom "I love you" before falling asleep. All these moments of pure, divine love that we feel in our heart, they send positive vibrations into the universe, and we have the power to multiply them. The Angel of Love who came to visit me and told me "Remember, you are loved" brought so much peace in me, it is indescribable; he made me feel in my core what Divine Love was. I can assure you, once you have a taste of it, you don't want to let it go and you want everybody to experience it!

I was not given this healing gift and I am not channeling love vibrations from higher spheres just for me. This is why I am writing this book now, to present this simple concept to people who are mainly too busy with their daily activities and their quest for more materialistic possessions, to stop and think about the real values we need to put our energy into if we want to survive, save our world, and reach global peace. These few words might resonates in some who will, in turn, spread these healing thoughts around them, thus making a difference in this new consciousness of oneness that we are currently experiencing, aside from the precepts and dogma taught and impounded on us by organized churches and governments. I am not the only one with such messages and desires for love and peace. I just hope that this book can help make more people aware of their own power toward this realization.

It is time we split apart from the dogmas and fears ingrained in us since our young age. We are in charge of our own reality; by changing our thoughts to positive thoughts, we make it happen. If we want love and peace on a global scale, we can start by each of us at the individual level, one change in behavior at a time. And the ripple effect of positive vibrations will spread immediately. Then, fears will disappear. The messages that the media and the governments send to control and entertain this fear will not affect people any longer. They will know that they are in charge of their own reality, one thought at a time, until a whole community of similar individuals will become the actors of this new paradigm of love. We should not be afraid to love, say it, and act upon it.

16

Scientific Vindication

As Dr. Emoto's experiments conclude, everything is alive. Green thumbs know that it helps to talk to plants to make them grow healthy and happy, but who would have imagined that talking to water could affect it? The power of words and the vibrations that go with them go a long way. I think that there is no better proof of it than Dr. Emoto's experiment.

While I do not need science to come and tell me that all things are alive, and that we are all one, I have noticed that some people resist accepting their new awareness of what their common beliefs would have completely refuted before. Those who claim they need to see before believing. Yet, when the feeling of oneness enters the soul, it cannot be dismissed. It is not something that you need to see to accept: it is a knowing, deep inside, which needs no explanation or vindication. But of course, the Universe knows it all, including the fact that some need a little bit of help to accept this new paradigm. Thus, it is not a coincidence if science is now giving proof of this oneness with the Universe. It will help scientific mind based people accept that what they cannot explain is of an ethereal nature, yet, totally fine to accept and possible. There is nothing wrong with accepting that we are part of the Universe, that we are Divine, and that there is more to it than what is seen and explainable. Science is now explaining the unexplainable; for those who need such vindication.

As I was about to finish writing my book, a friend of mine suggested a book that she had just started reading. She told me that I would probably find very interesting insights in it. So of course, I bought it immediately and read it.

Bruce Lipton, an internationally recognized cell biologist, former research professor at Stanford University, confirms in his book *"The Biology of Belief, Unleashing the Power of Consciousness, Matter and Miracles"*[12] what I felt at a spiritual level. Through experiments, which are the basis of science, he came to the conclusion that thoughts can affect reality. He talks about Epigenics, "the science of how environmental signals select, modify, and regulate gene activity" (p. 15).

In more scientific terms, he explains that "the cell engages in behavior when its brain, the membrane, responds to environmental signals. Every protein in our bodies is a physical/electromagnetic complement to something in the environment. Because we are machines made out of protein, by definition we are made in the image of the environment, that environment being the Universe, or to many, God." (p. 153). He also states that "the mechanics of the new science revealed the existence of our spiritual essence and our immortality" (p. 148). And that "The Universe is one indivisible, dynamic whole in which energy and matter are so deeply entangled it is impossible to consider them as independent elements" (p. 83). So, indeed, as Eric Pearl states in his book "The

Reconnection,"[13], it is truly about the restructuring of our DNA. Environmental influences can modify the genes we receive at birth and those modifications can be passed on to future generations (Lipton, p. 57).

As a result, if we all change our thoughts, not only can we receive immediate healing, but we can also benefit future generations. And we can certainly influence our environment through positive thinking that sends positive vibrations, what Bruce Lipton calls constructive interference, good vibes that positively affect us and our environment.

We then become co-creators of the world we want, and participate in the evolution of the Universe and of the human species through the thoughts and vibrations that emanate from us.

It is thus to the utmost importance that we, parents, pay particular attention to what our children are exposed to. If environmental influences can modify the genes we receive at birth, we can only hope that these influences be positive. Parents should make sure they are.

As I mentioned earlier, I feel that I am part of an harmonious orchestra. Bruce Lipton in his book talks about vibrations that create harmonic resonance. What he calls the quantum revolution is the scientific seal on spiritual matters. If we let go of fear, fear of change, fear of evolving, fear of being ourselves, even fear of happiness, which is entertained greatly on a daily basis by the media and the governments as a way of holding societies under their yokes, we can then reach this awareness that positive, loving thoughts is all it takes to be happy and healthy. If we let go of the ego, this ingrained master of the mind that tells you what you should believe according to the approved dogmas of societies, then, large doors will open to an unparalleled world of peace and love. If we accept that we are one with the Universe, we can open ourselves and radiate love toward everything in the Universe. No more competition, no more attachment to the materialistic, ephemeral world. We can all become part of this harmonious orchestra.

17

The Fifth World

When December 2012 approached, I knew that it was not the end of the world in the sense that the world would disappear, but the end of the world as we know it, spiritually speaking; I knew that it was a turning point, a shift to a new consciousness, a new paradigm. From a world of individuality, we were shifting to a world where individuals needed to come together as a community for a better world, where many would somehow realize that there is more to life than the world as we know it, and would open up to a higher level of consciousness that is beyond our little individual materialistic world of possession.

I am not saying that individual human beings would give up everything they had in the name of the wellbeing of the community, but that each individual would reassess their own wellbeing and take different routes toward a deeper connection with themselves, hence becoming more happy and releasing more positive vibrations.

As embodied spirits, we are to enjoy life, yet we should become more respectful of the gift of life. As individuals become more aware of this new paradigm and become more open to the concept of oneness, all together as individuals with the same purpose of being happy and living in peace, these individuals can create a community where only vibrations of love would resonate. This community encompasses the earth, and everything that makes it, including its inhabitants, not only us, humans, but every living being on earth. Though this statement seems to come from the era of the seventies and the hippy movement of peace and love on earth, I think that we have now reached a state on earth when we are ready for it.

The fifth world, as the Hopis[14] call it, is the time of a new reality, and we have begun the process of entering into it. It is a time when individualism, materialistic greed, destruction of the environment will bring a term to the world as we know it, and a new world where all will be loving and respectful will emerge.

Love applied to everything can bring this new reality. Vibrations of love not only have a direct effect, but also a ripple effect, thus multiplying it in intensity and scope.

It can become second nature to love and live according to this principle. Respect, love, honor, give thanks, all positive values that ensure our survival and happiness. From love and respect can only come peace. I know that it can sound utopic when we look at the current political situation all over the globe, yet I am convinced that we have the power to change things. Love of the trees, the streams, the birds, natural resources, ourselves, and each other. If we love everything that makes up our world, then we respect it and ensure its wellbeing, as we do for our family members and want all the best for them. I do not think that I was given the gift of being a planetary healer to keep this gift for myself and not spread the word of love I receive from the other side.

As a planetary healer, each time I receive a message about a catastrophe to happen, I think about the grid of networkers around the globe who receive the same messages and I join them in sending healing words of love to the earth, volcanos and mountains. I also think of my Sisters of the Stream who are sad to see the situation related to water on our planet. The message I received from them was very powerful; it was a plea for help that cannot be left unanswered.

In addition to healing the earth, we can also save it, protect it from further damage. We must take responsibility for our planet and respect it. It has now become an extremely time sensitive matter but it is not too late. We can all join our forces and spread these teachings of love and respect toward the earth. As I mentioned earlier about how our DNA evolves through our thoughts, we can have an even bigger impact on the future of the earth if we teach our children about respect and love of everything on this planet.

The more people will reach awareness of the effect they can have on the earth through positive thinking, respect and love, the better chances we have to heal the earth. It is all about energy. Have you entered a room where all attendants are gloomy and sour? You can feel that energy, a negative, heavy energy that drains all of yours if you stay too long. Now, if you go in a place where all are happy, you can feel the positive energy around, you can feel more light around, and the atmosphere itself is lighter. We can affect the world positively if we make sure our vibrations are positive wherever we go, whatever we do.

It is also time we realize that we are here for more than a world of possessions, that there is more to it than owning a nice house, a nice car, having all the latest electronic devices, watching all the latest movies on the largest screen and going on vacation to the nicest places on earth in the most expensive hotels with the nicest jewelries and cars waiting at the airport. If we do not protect the earth, the nicest of everything will be useless. We all need to work for the good of community, which is the earth. If we start looking at trees, streams, oceans and all that makes our world with respect, and we send them our loving thoughts, we can certainly reverse the destroying abusing effect that we have impounded on it for the past 150 years.

This requires that we expand our notion of love to everything that surrounds us. How can one destroy and disrespect something that one loves?

Native Americans knew how to respect resources. The coastal tribes of the Pacific Northwest honored the first salmon each year when it came back up stream and provided sustenance for the months to come. They knew the cycles of the earth and respected them. It is time we learn respect again.

I know that I received messages from the other side related to catastrophes about to happen to make me aware of my role as a participant in the healing process and I know that I am on call and that as these events require additional support and love, I will be called upon as a member of this group of planetary healers that are located everywhere around the globe on this grid of energetic connection, ready to send vibrations of love to the earth.

The first times when I was given such messages, I felt that I was tested, as if the Universe wanted to make sure that I was receiving such messages and finally knew what to do about it. Now, when I receive a message on an imminent earth movement, I acknowledge it and send deep, heartfelt thoughts of love to the earth and every cell on it and in it.

Based on the messages I receive from the other side about continuing what I am doing, I know that I am entrusted with a mission and I have to try and bring onboard as many people as possible to help protect the earth. I am part of an orchestrated symphony of earthly healers who are part of a huge concert that takes place all around the globe and that at some point, when all participants are attuned, and the time of the great concert will have come, we will all resonate in unison and connect all networks with vibrations of love. We can all become planetary healers. Sending thoughts of love is easy and available to all. We just need to open ourselves more, not be afraid, and participate in the global healing process of the earth and its inhabitants through love.

What I have learned over the years is certainly not to my own benefit. As I said earlier, the messages I receive are teachings I eventually need in order to help people I meet on my way or lead me in my missions. I believe that all the people we meet on our way are there for a reason. They are here to teach us lessons, so that we can grow in wisdom and love. I have learned a lot from people I have met along; I also learned to get rid of my ego through harsh experiences. Until one day, after having gone through all the layers of trauma I had experienced through many lifetimes, I learned to open within and find peace within, and I reached a level of oneness with the universe that is indescribable. I was part of the universe, part of the trees, the streams, the fish, the rain, the clouds; I was no longer attached to any materialistic item; I looked around me and consciously thought about the attachment I might feel to all these items, and I realized that these were items, objects, and what mattered was held within my core; I felt at peace within and I felt the Love of the Universe in my heart.

And I realized that I was a receiver and a transmitter. Messages about the earth, or from departed ones to embodied spirits, messages to random people I encounter on my path, I am not the one managing all these messages and encounters. The Universe makes it happen. All is directed by Higher Spheres. All these years of learning how to receive and transmit messages made me, I suppose, a good transmitter, which would explain why I receive healing requests. When I meet new people, I always wonder what will come out of it, but I do not manage any of it. It is far beyond me. Many times, I know even before we exchange words that the person sitting next to me will be part of my next learning experience, that one or both of us will get something out of it. I soon find out that I am a messenger of some kind, and when I talk to them, I know that the message that I give comes from the Universe, talking through me to help these people on their journey; I never know what is going to come out of it, how long it is going to take, it might be a few minutes encounter, or a few months exchange, but I know when the message is delivered and the communication with the other side is over.

It is like channeling a message, yet very surreptitiously, and without interfering whatsoever in each individual's journey. While such exchange happens, my words and conversation are directed by higher spirits and teachings I have received over the years. And each time, love is part of it.

What is rather new to me in terms of spiritual discovery and wisdom related to the earth and its protection has been known for centuries by ancient cultures and the Native Americans. And what is currently happening in our societies has been predicted in ancient times by many indigenous cultures around the world. I suppose the civilizing process led us astray from the real values we should base our lives on.

My American Indian Studies background had already brought me very insightful teachings, and while writing my book, I remembered prophecies described by various tribes; prophecies of the white men coming back to the native ways, prophecies of a new world of love and peace, and prophecies of messengers of love who will help give birth to the new world.

All these contacts with the other side, the message of love I receive from God and spirits from the other side, unexplainable feelings I have had since I was a little girl, an unexplainable connection to the other side as far as I can remember, assertive statements about the true values of life, shifts, trust in the Universe, knowing that all is well and that I am responding to my calling, knowing as well for a fact that all this comes from Higher Spheres, that it is all part of my journey for a better world. I am a messenger of love for a better world. I am a conduit, directly transmitting messages of love from Higher Spheres to inhabitants of the Fourth World. It is my mission and destiny and I fully embrace it. All my life I have felt more connected to the ethereal world than to the physical world. I guess that subconsciously, I felt that one day, my mission on earth would come out and I would finally understand my purpose.

If I can contribute to a better world, make people stop for a minute and realize that there is more to it than the daily life as we know it, that what matter is beyond the four walls of our house and comfort, and that tomorrow's happiness for future generations is in our hands, then I will be happy. I will have served my purpose. I want to be a midwife to the Fifth World, a world of peace, respect, and love for all, a world where we will have pure water, fish in the streams and green grass in the fields. I want our children and grand-children to live in peace and respect for each other and their environment.

We are constantly reminded of the love that comes from higher spheres, yet many times we are not open to it; we are too busy and self-centered to pay attention to these messages of love from beyond. We need to learn how to stop living in the express lane and start taking the time to appreciate everything that makes our world and protect it. We need to learn how to get rid of selfishness and greed. We need to start looking at ourselves as part of the Universe in which we live. We are all one. It is our duty to spread love around us, protect and respect the earth, and teach our children that what matters is love, pure, unconditional love for every cell on this planet and beyond.

Real Love Stories Never Have Endings

Real love stories never have endings. Let's hope that our love story with the earth expands and never ends. It is our duty to make it happen.

Beatrice Marx

Epilogue

So, little by little, I found confirmation that all made sense and is, in fact, explainable, scientifically, spiritually, and even extra-terrestrially. All these messages I have received over the years do, indeed, have a purpose. I now know that I am part of a big orchestra of loving participants who will all help bring in the Fifth world, the new paradigm, the new consciousness that we are all one, living and loving for the good of all.

Receiving and sending loving thoughts is available to all of us. We can all become planetary healers and bring love and peace on earth.

The love stories we feel for our earth, for our environment, for all who are gone, yet are still around and communicating, they indeed never have endings. The universe will change, but those in it, on the earthly plane and beyond, who love and trust, will still be around, always reassuring us that we are not alone, and that we are loved.

All that matters is Love.

Beatrice Marx

Notes

1. Nerburn, Ken (2006) *Chief Joseph and the Flight of the Nez Perce: The Untold Story of an American Tragedy*. HarperOne
2. Monahan, Glenn (2001*) Montana's Wild and Scenic Upper Missouri River*. Northern Rocky Mountains Books
3. Earth Observatory - Eruption of Grímsvötn Volcano – May 22, 2011 (http://earthobservatory.nasa.gov/NaturalHazards/view.php?id=50684)
4. USGS – Poster of the Eastern Turkey Earthquake of 23 October 2011 – Magnitude 7.1 (http://earthquake.usgs.gov/earthquakes/eqarchives/poster/2011/20111023.php)
5. Earth Observatory – Mount Tongariro Erupts. August 8, 2012 (http://earthobservatory.nasa.gov/IOTD/view.php?id=78791)
6. Reuters (August 11, 2012) Two quakes in Iran kill 180 and injure 1500 (Zahra Hosseinian) http://www.reuters.com/article/2012/08/11/us-iran-earthquake-idUSBRE87A08N20120811
7. Thereconnection.com
8. Masuru Emoto. Welcome to the World of Water http://www.masaru-emoto.net/english/water-crystal.html
9. Hammurabi was the sixth king of Babylon from 1792 BC to 1750 BC. His code of laws is the first written laws in recorded history. Each offense is accompanied with the corresponding punishment.

10. Hammurabi's Code of Laws – Preamble
    http://www.sacred-texts.com/ane/ham/ham04.htm
11. Padget, James (contributor) and Babinsky, Joseph (compiler) (2008) Messages – *Communications from the Spirit World – Love is the Heart and Soul of the Universe.* Publisher: Lulu.com
12. Lipton, Bruce, H. (2007) *The Biology of Belief: Unleashing the Power of Consciousness, Matter and Miracles.* Hay House
13. Pearl, Eric (2003) *The Reconnection; Heal Others, Heal Yourself.* Hay House
14. Federally recognized tribe of Native American people who live on the Hopi Reservation in northeastern Arizona

About the Author

Beatrice Marx is a French native who adopted the beautiful Pacific Northwest as her new home fifteen years ago.

She worked in the corporate world in executive positions for more than thirty years, both in Europe and in the United States, until she decided to go for her passions. She now spends her time creating quilts, translating books, writing and kayaking.

This book is her first book, based on real events and communications with the ethereal world.

www.beatricemarx.com

Beatrice Marx

www.ingramcontent.com/pod-product-compliance
Lightning Source LLC
Chambersburg PA
CBHW060831050426
42453CB00008B/653